SMALL CHANGE

SMALL CHANGE

ABOUT THE ART OF PRACTICE AND THE LIMITS OF PLANNING IN CITIES

Nabeel Hamdi

London • Sterling, VA

First published by Earthscan in the UK and USA in 2004

ISBN: 1-84407-005-0 paperback
1-84407-006-9 hardback

Typesetting by JS Typesetting Ltd, Wellingborough, Northants
Printed and bound in the UK by Cromwell Press Ltd, Trowbridge
Cover design by Holly Mann and Rachel Hamdi
Index by Indexing Specialists (UK)

For a full list of publications please contact:

Earthscan
8–12 Camden High Street
London, NW1 0JH, UK
Tel: +44 (0)20 7387 8558
Fax: +44 (0)20 7387 8998
Email: earthinfo@earthscan.co.uk
Web: **www.earthscan.co.uk**

22883 Quicksilver Drive, Sterling, VA 20166-2012, USA

Earthscan is an imprint of James and James (Science Publishers) and publishes in
association with WWF-UK and the International Institute for Environment and
Development

A catalogue record for this book is available from the British Library

Library of Congress Cataloging-in-Publication Data

Hamdi, Nabeel.
  Small change : the art of practice and the limits of planning in cities / Nabeel
Hamdi.
      p. cm.
  Includes bibliographical references and index.
  ISBN 1-84407-005-0 (pbk.) – ISBN 1-84407-006-9 (hardback)
    1. City Planning–Citizen participation. I. Title.

HT166.H356 2004
307.1'216–dc22
                                                              2004013710

Printed on elemental chlorine-free paper

FOR NADIA AND RYAN
AND FOR OLI

Born in Afghanistan, and of Iraqi parentage, Nabeel Hamdi qualified as an architect at the Architectural Association in London in 1968. He worked for the Greater London Council between 1969 and 1978, where his award-winning housing projects established his reputation in participatory design and planning. From 1981 to 1990 he was Associate Professor of Housing at the Massachusetts Institute of Technology (MIT), where he was later awarded a Ford International Career Development Professorship.

In 1997 Nabeel won the UN-Habitat Scroll of Honour for his work on Community Action Planning, and the Masters course in Development Practice that he founded at Oxford Brookes University in 1992 was awarded the Queen's Anniversary Prize for Higher and Further Education in 2001. He is currently Professor of Housing and Urban Development at Oxford Brookes University.

Nabeel has consulted on participatory action planning and the upgrading of slums in cities to all the major international development agencies, and to charities and NGOs worldwide. He is the author of *Housing without Houses* (IT Publications, 1995), co-author of *Making Micro Plans* (IT Publications, 1988) and *Action Planning for Cities* (John Wiley and Sons, 1997) and editor of the collected volume *Educating for Real* (IT Publications 1996).

CONTENTS

ACKNOWLEDGEMENTS

I am indebted to all those who, in different ways, have helped me to think through and write and produce this book. I would particularly like to acknowledge the efforts of Peter Townsend, who captioned the spirit of each chapter in the epigraphs he wrote; Hugo Slim, Brian Phillips and Charles Parrack for their encouragement, insights and suggestions during the drafting of the manuscript; Patama Roonrakwit for her contribution to Chapter 2; Prema Kumara and KA Jayaratne (Jaya) and others at Sevanatha in Colombo, Sri Lanka, for opening doors to people, projects and literature, and for their time and photographs; Malani Jayalath for her time and insights (and on whom Mela's story is based); and all those people I have talked to and interviewed in the streets and offices of the many countries I have visited. Thank you for your time and inspiration.

Thanks also to my students over the years, with whom I have been able to test and debate ideas and who, in different ways, have made significant contributions to the content of this book.

Thanks forever to Rachel Hamdi, my wife, for her long-standing support, and to her and Holly Mann for the design of the cover and the overall design ideas for the book. Thanks, too, to Holly for producing all the diagrams, except for Diagram A, which was drawn by Patama Roonrakwit. Thanks to Gabriel Townsend for editorial feedback; to Eddie Robbins for reading early proposals and, as always, helping to position my ideas; to Charlie and Jani Hampton, Hugo, Brian, Charles, Peter, Viv and all the others for our brainstorming sessions for ideas for titles, but especially to Teddy Hutton who, in a Paris café, suggested the title *Small Change*.

Finally, thanks to Viv Walker who typed up and put the manuscript together. Her editorial graphics and childhood recollections give the text, in part, its literary character. Her ability to invent words where mine were obscure opened doors to new theory – a world where most would fear to tread.

FOREWORD

This is a book about the process of 'development' in human societies. That statement itself calls for definition because of the unspoken assumptions underlying it. Inevitably the author has to devote his Introduction to an exploration of the question 'what is development?', and to the kind of answers that his students evolved, as well as to the impact of this exploration on their own personal development. It is almost as inevitable that the reader will be curious about the experiences of the book's author.

Many of us find that, more by chance than by intention, our working lives and activities are subdivided into periods that grow longer as we get older. Nabeel Hamdi is no exception to this general experience. After he qualified at the Architectural Association in London in 1970, where he made a special study of tropical architecture, he went to work for the Greater London Council (GLC) (which was subsequently abolished by Mrs Thatcher). During this period of its history, the GLC's Architects' Department was famous not only for the varieties of modern architecture it imposed upon the council's tenants, but also for the Hamdi experiment, which was known by the acronym PSSHAK (Primary Systems Support Housing and Assembly Kits). Influenced by the notion of 'support' structures proposed by the Dutch architect N J Habraken, Hamdi persuaded his employers to undertake two experiments in providing adaptable dwellings, where the layout of rooms and services could be varied to meet tenants' changing requirements.

He then spent a further decade, the 1980s, in the USA, mostly as a professor of housing in the Department of Architecture at the Massachusetts Institute of Technology (MIT), with its multinational atmosphere and outreach. He has continued to maintain contact with that lively, innovative department through his colleague there, Reinhard Goethert. Together they have collaborated on several key books. For example, in *Action Planning for Cities*[1] their devastating criticism of the mainstream ideology of planning is that its inflexibility, its passion to predict and control, its reliance upon a professional elite and its dependence on aid:

> *set it apart from the pluralistic, spontaneous, market-driven, entre-preneurial and serendipitous dynamics which shape cities in practice. The result is that few of the acclaimed benefits of planning reach the poor. And even when they do, it is at a cost in management, administration and other scarce resources which cannot long be sustained.*

Another vital figure from the Architectural Association in London (who, after years assisting squatters in Lima, Peru, was to be found at MIT in Boston promoting an alternative approach to housing) was John Turner. He formulated several principles of housing which, many years ago, I distilled from his writings and speeches as Turner's three laws of housing.[2]

Turner's first law, which I take from the book *Freedom to Build*, is significant in the context of this book:

> *When dwellers control the major decision and are free to make their own contribution to the design, construction or management of their housing, both the process and the environment produced stimulate individual and social well-being. When people have no control over, nor responsibility for, key decisions in the housing process, on the other hand, dwelling environments may instead become a barrier to personal fulfillment and a burden on the economy.*[3]

This carefully worded statement of a principle implies a fundamental change in attitudes from those which were current when it was formulated. And it also epitomizes the pioneering approach which, with a global network of acquaintance and of advisory visits, Nabeel Hamdi brought to his next appointment in 1990 as director of the Centre for Development and Emergency Planning (CENDEP) at Oxford Brookes University, attracting participants from around the world to a course which includes practical acquaintance with the dilemmas and responsibilities arising from temporary involvement in other people's lives and hopes. Membership of this annual course goes beyond architects and planners to include relief workers of all kinds, as well as nurses, lawyers and teachers, while beyond Europe and the USA, students have come to Oxford from Ecuador, Ethiopia, Sudan, Uganda, South Africa, India, Sri Lanka, Bangladesh, Thailand and Japan.

Another key book of Hamdi's, *Housing Without Houses*, explores the ideology of housing and the opinions of several alternative ideologists, such as Turner and Habraken, concluding that:

> *Building lots of houses for people and in places one does not know, where money is scarce and statistical information is unreliable, is neither an efficient nor an equitable way of solving housing problems, nor is it good design practice.*[4]

And he adds that this hypothesis is 'especially true when confronting economic, political and social climates that are always changing, and in contexts where a vast number of vested interests are always in conflict'. The fact that his second observation is true of most of the world as we know it adds to the importance of his first general statement, and the other themes of his book explore alternative approaches. The first is that of redefining design and planning as part of the process of *enablement*, and the second is the task of involving users in a process of participatory design. Other aspects of his exploration concerned the role of housing environments in improving family health, providing security and generating family income. And not the least of these new interpretations was the search for an alternative definition of the role of the visiting professional outsider.

Nobody believes any longer that the arrival by jet plane of a celebrity professional from the rich world has any relevance to people's lives in the poor world. There *has* been an advance, both in everyday wisdom and in sophisticated evaluation. And now, after many years of directing the Housing and Urban Development Programme at Oxford Brookes University, Nabeel Hamdi has set out his reflections on teaching and learning in this field of human activity.

Several of these reflections relate to the necessary shift in scale of the students' and experts' observation. I remember, many years ago, the American anthropologist Lisa Peattie talking about her puzzlement when she first settled in a Latin American city. The population was growing continually. The streets were thronged, but there seemed to be no equivalent expansion of the economy to employ and sustain this explosion of people. And yet, while she certainly saw poverty all around, no-one looked desperately ill-nourished and most people were shod. Slowly it dawned on her, as she observed the lives of the inhabitants of the barrio where she had chosen to live, that in addition to the official economy that figured in the statistics for employment and output and gross national product, there was a vast unofficial, invisible and unrecorded economy of a multitude of tiny enterprises and occupations among the city's unrecorded population, whose shanty settlements can evolve over time, given the right circumstances, into fully serviced suburbs. One of the tasks of the outsider is to be useful in helping to manipulate those circumstances.

The same shift in the scale of our thinking is necessary when we consider the economy. In 1966 George McRobbie and Fritz Schumacher instigated the formation of the Intermediate Technology Development Group. They wrote in its very first bulletin about the plight of the would-be purchasers of a simple tool: 'There used to be a bit of equipment you could buy for £20 to do a particular job. Now it costs £2000 and is fully automated, and we can't afford to buy it'. That was many years ago, and it explains why they accumulated a series of maxims:

If you want to go places, start from where you are.
If you are poor, start with something cheap.
If you are uneducated, start with something simple.
If you live in a poor environment, and poverty makes markets small, start with something small.
If you are unemployed, start with using your own labour power, because any productive use of it is better than letting it lie idle.

Each of these pieces of wise advice is reflected in the book before you, and the fact that they have been around for so long reinforces Nabeel Hamdi's experience that understanding the process of development demands a change of focus if the viewer from the rich world is to notice its component parts at all. This is why he has to draw our attention to the need 'to spot a pickle jar on someone's doorstep with pickles for sale' and to grasp the significance of the shop sign that reads 'Barber's Shop. We also Sell Bicycle Parts'.

In the concluding section of this book, Nabeel Hamdi turns to the lessons to be garnered from his years of training people in this field, of attempting to develop in the members of his course 'a kind of professional artistry which enables us to improvise and be informed', working as he says, 'somewhere between order and chaos'.

This involves skills of a different kind from those absorbed in the training of regular professions – whether architecture or nursing – and consequently the final chapters are devoted to exploring the styles of approach through which they can be acquired. Nabeel Hamdi's conclusions are the outcome of a professional lifetime's experience, but at the same time they are tentative because in this field, as the saying goes, 'circumstances alter cases'. If a uniquely successful approach to development practice existed, years of experience would have identified it. These chapters tell us what the author's encounters have taught him, and why they might be enlightening for us.

Colin Ward
Debenham, Suffolk
December 2003

INTRODUCTION: DESIGN, EMERGENCE AND SOMEWHERE IN-BETWEEN

*The only limit to our realization of tomorrow
will be our doubts of today.*

Franklin D Roosevelt

Each academic year we start our sessions with one of those class-room seminars on 'what is development?' – the kind of seminar that's never-ending and impossible to conclude but which gets everyone thinking. Most times the response is predictable. Development is whatever you want it to be depending on your politics and ideology: economic growth, rights, freedom, livelihoods, good governance, knowledge, power – all of which are often interspersed with words like 'integration', 'sustainability', 'empowerment', 'partnerships', 'participation', 'community', 'democracy', or 'ethics'. In combination, all the ideals they invoke offer us hope for building a better and fairer world and, for the poor majority around the world, a better deal.

Sometimes, to liven things up, I select a combination of words from Robertson's lexicon of buzzwords arranged in four columns of 14 words each, generating in total some 38,000 development options: something like, 'development is: democratically (column A) structured (column B) institutional (column C) involvement (column D)'; and then we discuss the outcomes.[1] Each of my student groups will have a different interpretation of what it all means – a witness to the ambiguity of the language and the jargon of development which we try to dispel or come to terms with at the earliest stage.

Occasionally, someone brightens things up and offers us an alternative view. Last year someone ventured an idea that got us thinking very differently. Development, he said, happens when people, however poor in money, get together, get organized, become sophisticated and go to scale. It happens when they are savvy and able to influence or change the course of events or the order of things locally, nationally or even globally – or are themselves able to become that order or part of it. Development, he said, (as he pointed to his copy of Kaplan's *The Development Practitioner's Handbook*)[2] is that stage you reach when you are secure enough in yourself, individually or collectively, to become interdependent; when 'I' can emerge as 'we', and also when 'we' is inclusive of 'them'. His assumption was enduring and simple. Getting organized is the foundation of all the other developmental goals we have set; it is the essence of good governance and of sustainable work; it empowers and opens doors; it makes you money and wins you respect.

I began to wonder what this could mean in practice and what theory of practice was implied. It got me thinking again about Steven Johnson's book on 'emergence' and his account of Keller, Lee and Nakagaki's research into slime mould behaviour and the application of mathematics to the understanding of biology.[3] Their research was a part of the scientific search for an understanding of how simple and mostly independent cells, under the right conditions, come together and emerge as a larger more sophisticated organization, not led by a single brain and without the help of an executive branch, much in the way in which the highly sophisticated and informal sector works in cities.

Johnson reports that in August 2000, Nakagaki, a Japanese scientist, had trained the slime mould (that brownish stuff you find in your garden) to find its way through a maze. He placed some food at two of the maze's exits. The slime mould solved the problem of the maze and found the food. But if the mould had no brain and no executive cell, how was it able to do this?

Scientists had discovered in the late 1960s that each cell of the slime mould relays signals to its neighbours by emitting a substance called acrasin, which enables cells to aggregate and form clusters. 'It' becomes 'they' in response to changes in the environment or in their search for food, and all without some big shot giving instructions! The slime mould, they found, '…oscillates between being a single creature and a swarm',[4] between independence and interdependence.

Sociologists have their own way of describing the ying and the yang of 'I' and 'we'. In his discussion on sociability, Georg Simmel, an innovator in contemporary sociology, put it this way:

> [T]he individual has to fit himself into a whole system and live for it: that, however, out of this system values and enhancement must flow back to him, that the life of the individual is but a means for the ends of the whole, the life of the whole but an instrument for the purpose of the individual.[5]

The point that the scientists and Simmel are making is that organic systems, in nature and in society, exhibit patterns – recognized in the informal cities of everywhere – where problems are solved by drawing on a variety of information from the multitude of small, relatively simple and local elements, rather than from some power elite or single brain (which the early researchers assumed guided the behaviour of the mould). There was no prior planning, but there was an effective system of communication that enabled the slime mould to act spontaneously and to self-organize in response to need (or aspiration), from the bottom up. This ability to organize and become sophisticated, to move from one kind of order to another higher level of order, scientists call 'emergence'.

In many respects, emergence and development – at least the kind ventured in class earlier – share similar characteristics. They both include what Danah Zohar calls 'quantum systems', which are self-organizing and indeterminate. Their individual bits or cells:

> ... have no fully fixed identity until they are in relationship. This gives the quantum system maximum flexibility to define itself as it goes along. It co-creates with its environment. All of nature's complex systems are at their most creative when they are delicately poised between fixedness and unfixedness – poised at the edge of chaos.[6]

But development and emergence – the kind exhibited in nature – differ in at least two significant respects. First, development, like all human processes, needs designed structure with rules and routines that provide continuity and stability and that offer a shared context of meaning and a shared sense of purpose and justice. To these structures we 'give up some of our liberty in order to protect the rest'.[7] The question facing practice is: how much structure will be needed before the structure itself inhibits personal freedom, gets in the way of progress, destroys the very system which it is designed to serve, and becomes self-serving? At what point does it disable the natural process of emergence, with all its novelty and creativity? '[S]kilful [practitioners] understand the interdependence between design and emergence. They know that in today's turbulent … environment, the challenge is to find the right balance between the creativity of emergence and the stability of design.'[8]

In the second instance of divergence, emergence in nature differs from development in the ways in which collectives form and become communities. There are at least five different and overlapping ways in which communities form, which we will observe in the examples in Part 2. These include communities of culture or place, communities of interest, and communities of practice and resistance. Each will differ in its constituency, in its value systems, in its codes of conduct, and in its beliefs and aspirations. Each will vary in its terms of engagement with partners. Some will compete for power and authority and others may be in open conflict.

This shifting balance between constantly competing levels, between the freedom and rights of individuals and the order of collective responsibility, between large-scale organizations and small ones, between public life (we) and private life (I), as well the differences between kinds of community, continues to preoccupy social scientists, architects, planners and economists. It is at the heart of a new activism that today can revitalize practice with new purpose. It offers new roles and responsibilities to practitioners. It enables us to cultivate afresh the ideals of community, participation, and governance, and to reconceptualize the planning process itself.

Driving it all, and throughout this book, is a simple, yet still challenging, premise: intelligent practice builds on the collective wisdom of people and organizations on the ground – those who think locally and act locally – which is then rationalized in ways that make a difference globally. In the language of 'emergence', 'it's better to build a densely interconnected system with simple elements and let the more sophisticated behaviour trickle up.'[9] In this respect, good development practice facilitates emergence; it builds on what we've got and with it goes to scale.

It follows, therefore, that in order to do something big – to think globally and act globally – one starts with something small and one starts where it counts. Practice, then, is about making the ordinary special and the special more widely accessible – expanding the boundaries of understanding and possibility with vision and common sense. It is about building densely interconnected networks, crafting linkages between unlikely partners and organizations, and making plans without the usual preponderance of planning. It is about getting it right for *now* and at the same time being tactical and strategic about *later*. This is not about forecasting, nor about making decisions about the future. But it is about the long range, about making sure that one plus one equals two or even three, about being politically connected and grounded, and about disturbing the order of things in the interests of change.

Practice disturbs. It can and does promote one set of truths, belief systems, values, norms, rituals, powers and gender relations in place of others. It can impose habits, routines and technologies that may lead to new and unfamiliar ways of thinking, doing and organizing, locally, nationally and even globally. It may do this intentionally because existing structures have become malignant, or because they could work more effectively if they were to change, or because there is no order – no sophistication where it is needed. It may also do so in the interests of one power elite over another to induce internationally a new global order. In all these respects, practice – that skilful art of making things happen; of making informed choices and creating opportunities for change in a messy and unequal world – is a form of activism and demands entrepreneurship.

Practice sparks the process by which small organizations, events and activities can be scaled up. This can happen in various ways: quantitatively, where programmes get bigger in size and money; functionally, through integration with other programmes and other organizations both formal and informal; politically, where programmes and communities can wield power and can become part of the governance of cities; and organizationally, where the capacity to be effective increases and becomes sophisticated and influential – at which point it becomes a higher order of organization.[10] Emergence and going to scale are, therefore, complementary processes: practice is a catalyst to both.

This philosophy of 'acting in order to induce others to act', of offering impulses rather than instructions, and of cultivating an environment for change from within, starts on the ground and often with small beginnings which have 'emergent' potential – a bus stop, a pickle jar, a composting bin, a standpipe – as we shall see in Part 2 of this book.

From these small and often simple beginnings, with all their practical objectives of improving housing, health and education, emerges an agenda of reforms to policy, legal frameworks and standards which help to build social capital, promote social integration and gender equality, reduce dependency, unlock resources and build livelihoods:

> *Shared ownership of the development agenda is seen as key to its sustainability. . . [P]ublic, private and civic roles are being reconceptualized and reshaped in both economics and social policy: the best route to problem solving lies through partnership.*[11]

Problem-seeking and problem-solving in these settings demand that we think at once serially, associatively and holistically. Danah Zohar calls these three kinds of thinking the brain's intellect, heart and spirit. With the intellect we define goals, set tasks, evaluate the evidence, collect facts, search for precedent and search for logic. Then there is the brain's heart – that form of associative or parallel thinking that finds associations between things, events, people and structures, and that taps experience, learning by trial and error. And, importantly, there is the brain's spirit – imaginative, intuitive, insightful, creative, unwilling to accept old paradigms as given, inventing new categories of thought, being holistic, finding new ways of making one and one add up to three, and finding a new path when 'our rule-bound and habit-bound thinking can't cope'.[12]

It is here that imagination is as important as knowledge or skill when deciding on professional intervention. 'Begin with imagination', said the Nobel prize winning author Jose Saramago – 'but from then on let reason prevail'.[13] Working in the slums and shanties of any major city in the South, it takes imagination to plant the seed of the idea of community around bus stops and water points, and to craft these creatively, with reason, as centres of community life; or to spot in someone else's waste the implicit opportunities for enterprise, entrepreneurship and new forms of partnership to manage waste and conserve energy. It takes imagination to adopt a local cricket club as a partner in promoting social development in an otherwise divided community; or to spot a pickle jar on someone's doorstep with pickles for sale and then expand the source of this produce through a community garden, managed by the elderly and involving children as partners, for promoting healthy living. It takes imagination to turn a rickshaw into a school bus, offering services and security for children in a settlement that is otherwise inaccessible to services, and contracted by the local authority, thereby generating employment and creating more partnerships, both public and private, formal and informal. It takes imagination to see the pirating of electricity as an opportunity for privatizing a utility around a single pylon, or to see a standpipe with its intermittent supply of water as means of generating income, creating a community fund out of surplus tariff revenue, empowering women and promoting health awareness.

And further in this example, it takes more imagination combined with reason to convince the municipal authorities to seek new partnerships with this, by now established and sophisticated, community organization, and to change the legal structure of rights so that other communities who lack entitlement can benefit as well. In time we might encourage a new horizontal structure of water management networks which become an integral part of the way cities manage their supply – a new institutional arrangement which everyone recognizes as useful and profitable; something both practical and tactical. It takes imagination to convince a multinational corporation to partner with a community organization to fight fire and reduce the risks of man-made or natural hazards and disasters, or to negotiate debt conversion between governments that shares out the benefits of debt relief with disenfranchised community groups in a new global alliance inclusive of grassroots organizations, designed to reduce poverty, promote social justice and save the environment. In all these ways we recognize in practice the important dialectic between top-down planning, with its formal and designed laws and structures, and bottom-up self-organizing collectivism – those 'quantum and emergent systems' which Jane Jacobs argued long ago give cities their life and order.[14]

The examples in this book will show that skilful and creative practice in these interdependent settings hinges on our capacity to handle the unexpected in controlled but creative ways, and on chance encounters and chance learning. It depends on the ability to improvise as we stumble upon good ideas and as problems manifest themselves unpredictably, and on upside-down thinking, and on making mistakes and being reflective.

'Although we sometimes think before acting', said Don Schon, 'it is also true that in much of the spontaneous behaviour of skilful practice, we reveal a kind of knowing which does not stem from a prior intellectual operation.'[15]

This kind of knowing is less normative, less easy to standardize in its routines and procedures, less tolerant of data-hungry study, and less reliant on statistics or systems analysis. Consistency, it will be shown, is the 'hobgoblin of simple minds' rather than a measure of professional competency. There are few sacred prototypes to follow, no best practices for export, no brand names that guarantee quality. Instead, approximation and serendipity are the norm – the search for scientific precision is displaced in favour of informed improvisations, practical wisdom, integrated thinking and good judgement based on a shared sense of justice and equity, and on common sense.

These competencies, we will see, combined with a good measure of idealism and pragmatism, enable practitioners to move easily and creatively from the high ground of global issues into the swamp of the everyday with its small beginnings and seemingly irrational short cuts to survival and success – to the strategic setting of national policy development, into the board rooms of development banks and multinationals – seeking inspiration from all levels with the moral imperative to solve problems and change minds and in ways which make a difference and more, on a scale that counts. This book is about practice, about emergence, about disturbance and about development activism working in the informal city of everywhere. The stories I tell are based on my own experiences and those of others, collected from countries worldwide. Each story embodies in its own right a set of principles and ideas important to practice. I have combined them into a single narrative in the imaginary city of anywhere because, together, they tell of the continuum of development and offer a framework for process and planning.

The title, *Small Change*, captures three important principles that recur throughout: 'small' because that's usually how big things start; 'change', because that's what development is essentially about; and 'small change', because this can be done without the millions typically spent on programmes and projects.

In structuring the text I have avoided the more usual and sometimes prescriptive logic of planning sequence, recommendations and bullet point summaries, preferring instead to convey something of the spirit, meaning, entrepreneurship and artistry of practice in an attempt to try things out and make things happen. It is a book you read rather than study, and it is organized in three parts.

Part 1 sets the scene. It is an introduction to the spatial and political arenas in which our examples in Part 2 are set. It introduces key issues and raises questions based first on observations that later will need answers. It outlines the hierarchy of dependency between organizations at local, urban, national and global levels. It reveals the ambiguities and contradictions that are a context for, rather than a barrier to, practice. It reviews the new global order, driven by the forces of globalization and the neo-liberal agenda of the Washington Consensus, and argues that despite some benefits, the evidence overwhelmingly points to social, economic and environmental harm endemic to poor countries and their poor majority that has resulted from this new order. Aid, we conclude, keeps the belief of development alive but does little for development itself.

In Part 2 each section and each story offers a window on the intelligence of the informal city – how small beginnings can be carefully crafted into large programmes, and how emergence can be encouraged and structures designed. Whereas Part 1 is pessimistic, Part 2 is optimistic. From the early struggles with eviction, the crisis of resettlement and the daily uncertainty of risk from fire, flood or poor sanitation, we see the informal, progressive and spontaneous emergence of new ways of solving problems and, in time, of a new order as people get organized. As this capacity to organize into collectives and networks wins recognition and commitment more broadly, so we see these same collectives become communities as they develop their own rituals, meanings and rules of conduct around work, a common purpose or an ideal. And as they begin to achieve their purpose, however small or local, and make gains in the novel and transformative ways which they always do, through partnerships, cooperation and learning, so they gain power and status and go to scale. They win respect and dignity and a place in the governance of cities. They become intelligent because they become organized and connected.[16] They become sophisticated.

We will see how street-level enterprises and small organizations can become integral to citywide programmes involving city-level and even national-level organizations, including the city public works department in waste management and fire services, the university and its various departments in health provision and design, or the department of education promoting education for development triggered by Tandia's pickle jar. Later, novel policy initiatives might emerge for creating organizations run in close collaboration with all stakeholders, for making contracts with communities, and for new forms of partnership and governance based on networks, not hierarchies.

Experience everywhere confirms how all these small beginnings – this seemingly ad-hoc and makeshift landscape of loose parts and organizations – give cities their ordered complexity, which is at once flexible, durable and, as we have seen, infinitely resourceful. They offer fast and ingenious short-cuts to goods and services and 'a vitality of energy and social interaction that depends critically upon diversity, intricacy and the capacity to handle the unexpected in controlled but creative ways'.[17] We will see how practice and practitioners 'using the power of [their] authority to empower others',[18] can nurture this process – or sometimes how they can disable it. We will learn how skilful practice can trigger the emergence of novelty and organization; how it can help build an architecture of opportunity for rediscovering community, building networks and stronger organizations, and making money – for communication and learning to flourish, and for new partnerships to be explored. In so doing, we enable people to find new ways of doing, thinking and relating in response to everyday problems which one takes for granted – breaking down barriers; optimizing not maximizing. These are all qualities of leadership in practice and for development – a new openness for dialogue and learning.

Each story is analysed critically to make explicit the values, ethics, tools, techniques, methods, roles and relationships implicit in what it takes to be competent, imaginative and skilful in practice. Each story is interconnected – the whole offers a profile of practice in relation to the design and implementation of urban programmes.

Part 3 is about learning. In particular, it is about becoming both skilful and wise, about being reflective, and bridging the gap between doing and learning, theory and practice, class work and street work. We draw lessons from our experience in Part 2 and, in particular, in relation to the roles, relationships, behaviour and values in respect to people, organizations and events we have encountered. The first two sections are about planning and governance. The first deals with the planning process and with work habits. In it, I make the case for working backwards: reversing the order of survey–analyse–plan and, instead, working to plan–analyse–survey, then reflect, then plan–analyse–survey; cyclically and progressively. The second section is about governance and, in particular, a form of governance based on networks, not hierarchies, where users become partners in the services society provides, where 'enterprise is governed and run by and for its members' through mutual cooperation.[19] It's an inside-out organization where the whole is held together by the parts, where design and emergence are balanced.

In the third section I review the learning environment in which we might nurture wisdom, as well as the skills and competencies we need in practice. I will argue that mistrust, defensiveness, jargon, abstraction and intellectual competitiveness still dominate academia. The advancement of belief systems takes precedence over critical thinking. Knowledge is valued more than experience or understanding. Rationality and factual evidence are more rewarded than creativity because they are easier to measure. All of these things are a barrier to learning. They are anti-developmental.

Finally, and by way of summary, I offer a code of conduct based on my own experiences and the experiences and advice of others:

Ignorance is liberating
Start where you can: never say can't
Imagine first: reason later
Be reflective: waste time
Embrace serendipity: get muddled
Play games, serious games
Challenge consensus
Look for multipliers
Work backwards: move forwards
Feel good

PART I
THE SETTING

'ZENOBIA, A CITY IN ASIA, HAS HOUSES MADE OF BAMBOO AND ZINC, WITH many platforms and balconies placed on stilts at various heights, crossing one another, linked by ladders and hanging belvederes, with barrels storing water, weather vanes, jutting pulleys, fish poles and cranes.

No-one remembers what need, command or desire drove Zenobia's founders to give their city this form, as the buildings are constructed on pilings that sit over dry terrain. But what is certain is that if a traveller asks an inhabitant of Zenobia to describe his vision of a happy life, it is always a city like Zenobia that he imagines, with its piling and suspended stairways, a Zenobia perhaps aflutter with banners and ribbons, quite different from the original but always derived by combining elements of that first model.

However, it is pointless to try to decide whether Zenobia is to be classified among happy cities or among the unhappy. It makes no sense to divide cities into these two species, but rather into a different two: those that through the years and the changes continue to give form to their desires and those in which desires either erase the city or are erased by it.'

Italo Calvino, *Le Cita Invisibili*, 1972[1]

I

STREET WORK AND DEV-TALK: WHO CONTROLS THE TRUTH?

In which we get a view from below and another from above; and some idea of what it's like to meddle with the muddle in the middle.

Imagine one of those largely improvised and fast-changing cities that regularly feature in UN ledgers and annual human development reports with alarming statistics on poverty, child mortality, environmental degradation, rates of urbanization and political instability. Its population is growing at some 6 per cent annually – its supply of housing services and utilities has long ceased to match demand through formal channels, public or private. Because of this rampant urbanization, its centre will be choked with traffic and traffic fumes, with pavement dwellers and illegal construction; its periphery will sprawl uncontrollably with formal and informal settlements, markets and business parks. Productivity will be severely constrained by inadequate infrastructure, overly restrictive regulations, unenforceable policies on land reform, tariffs and taxation, and by institutional corruption. Its poor majority will earn less than $2 a day and some less than $1 a day – most of whom will be unable or unwilling to pay for services. Some 30 per cent of its population will lack safe water; one in five will have no access to health care. And because its people are poor, its local government will also be poor, because collecting taxes or tariffs for services will cost more than they could hope to collect. Investment in education, shelter, water and sanitation will be limited without aid, despite the added burden that aid will place on national economics. Therefore, at best, only between 20 per cent and 50 per cent of all solid waste will be effectively disposed of and half its housing stock will be in slum or other informal settlements, most of which are on marginal and unsafe land – on dump sites, railways or canal easements, on landfill, unstable hillsides, under bridges, along fire breaks, on roof tops, in cemeteries, behind chemical factories or on flood plains. Gender and other inequalities – age, disability, ethnicity and class – will be accentuated in the competition for credit, houses, land, jobs, education, health care, transportation, safe water and sanitation.

Walk down any street and quickly you will get a sense of what the issues are, of how all the aid and planning, and non-planning, appears on the ground; of what a development agenda might begin to look like. Spot, for example, the buckets in line at a standpipe that delivers water for two or three hours a day (if you are lucky); observe the uncleared rubbish and blocked drains; the public latrines, unusable because they were broken or because they were locked in case they did get broken; and the pirating of electricity and water. Track down the hosepipes to those who do have water, or the electrical line to those who are connected – middle men selling on water and electricity at prices much higher than those charged by the local utility company. Observe the children operating with difficulty hand pumps at the well, the women walking great distances with water buckets, and ask yourself: who manages water? And then, who designs hand pumps and decides acceptable carrying distances? Look down the narrow alleyways, observe the paper, card and timber scraps, plastic sheeting, cloth and other recycled material used for house building, and ask: what happens when there is a fire? How do children get to school, given that the school bus could never gain access to these narrow streets? In any case, who owns what, who is renting to whom, who does what? Observe all the enterprises – people repairing bicycles, making aluminium sheets from soda cans or shoe soles from old rubber tyres, working as scribes or running coffee houses, and ask: what would help their enterprise along? Do they need credit, and if so, where do they get it from? How do they establish markets? Then observe how, in every nook and cranny, under stairwells, between houses, in every leftover space, people put up small kiosks for selling goods and services, small shelters for mechanics or a single washing machine advertising laundry services. And in the street, every evening, an informal market appears that, by midnight, disappears again.

Then pop into any one of the houses you will pass. Look at the priority that people attach to income rather than comfort. How much of the dwelling will be devoted to home-based enterprise, how and where do people cook, eat and sleep? Talk to the family about the money they receive from family members overseas, about ownership, about belonging, about the value of house as 'social honour' and you will hear familiar stories: the lack of credit for business or education; the clinic that's too far and, when you do get there, you have no entitlement to treatment or medicine because you have no legal status, no citizenship; the insecurity because of threat of eviction and, with it, the lack of status and entitlement; how children fear using pit latrines because they are dark, because they are designed for adults and because the children fall into the pit; all the divisions between caste, and between newcomers and long-term residents; between the entrepreneurs and the less skilled; between men and women and, again, ask yourself: what is community? What sense of commitment can there be to any long-term planning? Who will likely work with whom in managing services or utilities, building houses or schools, paving roads, running the school bus? Talk to the man who runs around the market with his basket and trolley delivering flowers and vegetables, who makes some 100 trips a day, walking some 2 kilometres, who lays his trolley horizontally at night in some street corner and uses it as a bed. How much does he make? To whom does he pay rent for the trolley? Who does he sell to? Where are his family? How is the trolley cartel organized and could it become a partner in any future work?

Walk into one of the housing blocks, climb the dark, damp, crumbling stairway, observe the network of hosepipes dangling every which way, running from one floor to another, the tangled wires of electricity. The higher up you climb, the lower your status, the cheaper the rent. Enter one of the apartments: two rooms, with a small kitchen and bathroom attached, occupied by a family of six; a mezzanine roughly built for storage; on the balcony – buckets for storing water, carried up every morning because even when there is mains water, the pressure is too low to find its way to the fifth floor. The father is a parking attendant at a local hotel, the sons work in the fish market – where the buses stop, the hub to the neighbourhood. They pay rent to someone they don't know, but that someone gives them security and has done so for 20 years.

Up on the roof – a settlement in its own right – there are roof-top squatters with houses built from bits of wood, tarpaulin sheets and other scavenged materials. There are shops, a small nursery, public latrines connected to rainwater down pipes – the smell of sewage everywhere. They also pay rent to a woman who looks after their interests, who lives on the roof but seems to be well-connected – a partner maybe.

All this in a country laden with debt and in an international environment dominated by aid conditionality and market protectionism. It is here that all the hardship and squalor can be explained, where the barriers to development can be found. The national government will have been 'lectured on good governance and principles of participation by countries that have an undemocratic stranglehold on international institutions and who, through the international aid regime, consistently undermine local structures, capacities and accountability'.[2] The statistics are startling. It will be a country paying some 40 per cent of its national revenue on debt servicing and repayments and unable, therefore, to meet its commitment to proper health care, education and the rest. It will have been undergoing debt restructuring in order to meet its repayment commitment, to promote economic growth and eradicate poverty. There will have been tax cuts, deregulation of markets, a reduction in the role of government and, where possible, its elimination altogether – privatize where you can. Results everywhere have been harmful: the collapse of the internal purchasing power of economies; the outbreak of famines; bread riots; closing of clinics and schools in favour of private institutions; charging of fees that have reduced attendance at schools; charges on medical and hospital attendance, causing a drop in both; general breakdown in curative and preventative care as a result of lack of medical equipment and supplies, poor working conditions and low pay of medical personnel.[3]

For every dollar it borrows, the government will be returning some four dollars to donor country banks in reverse aid and paying some 15 per cent above market rates for goods and services because of conditionality tied to aid – a direct subsidy globally to exporters in OECD countries of some $2 billion a year. This flow of capital finances the deficit of countries in the North. According to the New Economics Foundation '[T]he US now needs about $4 billion a day to finance its current account deficit. This reversal of flows is one of the main features of the phenomenon of globalization, and explains in part, flows of capital away from developing countries and subsequent impoverishment':[4]

> *Among the big donors, the US has the worst record for spending its aid budget on itself – 70 per cent of its aid is spent on US goods and services. And more than half is spent in middle-income countries in the Middle East. Only $3 billion a year goes to South Asia and sub-Saharan Africa.*[5]

As Julius Nyerere, President of Tanzania, said many years ago, 'Should we really let our people starve so that we can pay our debt?'[6] On top of it all, and despite the claim for free markets, there will be severe restrictions placed on trade through taxes, tariffs and quotas, which will have reduced exports. Clothing, our case country's second largest export, will be taxed by the US at 19 per cent (imports from Japan, France or Germany are charged between 0 per cent and 1 per cent). Raw cocoa beans can be exported to the EU and USA without tax, but if the source country processes these it will be charged more: butter at 10 per cent, cocoa powder at 15 per cent and chocolate at 20 per cent – all in order to protect local markets.[7]

And then there are subsidies. Rich countries also spend some $1 billion a day on subsidies to farmers that will undercut prices worldwide. In the US, its 25,000 cotton farmers receive more than $3 billion each year in support. The international cotton advisors' committee estimates that these subsidies lower world prices by about 25 per cent.[8]

Regionally, the share of world exports will have dropped from 1.2 per cent to 1 per cent. Overall, and despite the claims of growth and prosperity, what we find is 'a position where resources move from the poor to the rich and pollution moves from the rich to the poor'.[9] It was Richard Nixon, after all, who said in 1968 'Let us remember that the main purpose of American aid is not to help other nations but to help ourselves'.[10]

Globally, poor countries, who hold 40 per cent of the world population, will receive 3 per cent of the world's income in trade. Although the volume of exports from Africa increased by 25 per cent in the 1980s, the deterioration in terms of trade has meant that its earnings have fallen by 30 per cent since 1981:[11]

> *With the creation of the World Trade Organization (WTO) in the mid-1990s, economic globalization, characterized by 'free trade' was hailed by corporate leaders and politicians as a new order that would benefit all nations, producing worldwide economic expansion where wealth would trickle down to all. However, it soon became apparent to increasing numbers of environmentalists and grassroots activists that the new economic rules established by the WTO were manifestly unsustainable and were producing a multitude of interconnected fatal consequences – social disintegration, a breakdown of democracy, more rapid and extensive deterioration of the environment, the spread of new diseases and increasing poverty and alienation.[12]*

Still, despite various international targets, some 1.2 billion people worldwide are without safe drinking water and 2.9 billion lack adequate sanitation. The average income of 54 countries declined in the 1990s. Every day 30,000 children die from preventable disease; 500,000 women a year die in pregnancy or childbirth. In the 1990s, 13 million children were killed by diarrhoea. Human development, measured by the human development index (a combination of income, life expectancy and literacy), fell in 21 countries during the 1990s. One in five adults cannot read and 98 per cent of these are in countries of the developing South – two-thirds of these are women.[13]

The news, however, is not all bad. The Department for International Development (DfID) claims that many targets set within the millennium development goals to improve quality of life are being met. For example, nine out of ten children now go to primary school (20 years ago it was eight in ten); infant mortality has fallen from ten deaths in every 100 births to six. Six out of every ten people have access to clean water compared with four in ten 20 years ago. Overall, the target to halve the number of the world's poor by the year 2015 is within range – so they say.[14]

Meanwhile, globally, the environmental outlook is bleak, despite some gains. Every year, an estimated 6 million hectares of land in the world turns to desert – an area equivalent to nearly twice the size of Belgium. 'At least 15 per cent of the Earth's surface is already degraded by human activity'[15] by industry, urbanization, deforestation and overgrazing. Weather-related disasters that affected 147 million people a year, on average, 10 years ago, now affect some 211 billion people a year. Forty per cent of the world is short of fresh water; in 30 years this will rise to 50 per cent. Yet the average person in the UK uses 30 gallons per day compared with an average of 2 gallons used by people in the developing countries of the South; New Yorkers use 68 litres a day, a Kenyan 4 litres a day. Half of the world's rivers are seriously depleted and polluted. About 60 per cent of the 227 biggest rivers are disrupted by dams and other engineering works.[16]

Worldwide, there will be an average of $56 billion of aid a year pumped into a variety of development projects and programmes, decided upon largely by a donor community according to their national interests and pre-set global agendas. That donor community is made up of UN and trade organizations, development banks, government agencies and multinationals, with their NGO partners and their 100,000+ consultants who, with all their local counterparts, deliver technical assistance to some of the 1.5 billion people living in absolute poverty.

There might be housers wanting to build cheap, environmentally sustainable houses, to upgrade slums – promoting small enterprise and appropriate technologies; municipal engineers with their concerns for public health and safety, looking to reduce the burden on their administration through private-sector partnerships; and community builders whose prime interest is community organizing. Then there will be NGOs of all sizes, advocating global democracy with their humanitarian charters, championing the cause of the disenfranchised, the livelihoods of the poor and human rights; each with their special interests, some reformist, others confrontational, each lobbying, advocatory, mediating, networking, capacity building and strengthening civil society. And in response to growing criticisms about their legitimacy, many will be seeking to be more representative, more transparent and more accountable:

> *In the last 10 years, NGOs realized they had to account differently for what they did, they also had to account for what they said. This sort of 'voice accountability' had to respond to two areas of interrogation: the voracity of what they said and the authority with which they spoke. Although obviously linked, questions of voracity were essentially empirical (can you prove it?) while questions of authority were essentially political (from where do you derive your power to speak?).*[17]

There are some 28,900 international NGOs and 20,000 transnational networks. There are more than 1200 NGOs in Nepal alone, more than 1 million in India and 210,000 in Brazil. Their exponential growth has been explained in three ways: (1) as a counterforce to the Washington Consensus, arguing for a stronger social and institutional structure in addition to growth, markets and trade; (2) they are cost-effective in public relations where NGOs bring with them legitimacy and social or environmental responsibility to agency and corporate projects; (3) they give voice to civil society in global governance where trust in government has been undermined by the narrow objectivity of globalization and its neo-liberal theorists.[18]

Then there is the donor community, itself vying for power and authority, concerned with liberalizing markets, restructuring national economies, disbursing and managing money, and seeking to do this in ways which reduce poverty, save the environment, reform governments and build civil society. For example, there might be the port authority that owns large parcels of land in and around the city or the military whose officers own significant tracts of land adjoining your project area and who will want to safeguard and enhance their property values. There will be the housing bank, through which funds for housing will be channelled and which will depend on a good record of cost recovery in order to secure more aid money next time; and the planning authority, whose chairman is predicted to be the next national president. He will want quick, visible and politically safe projects which will give him votes and which will win his authority more political clout.

And, of course, there will be the community. They will not be homogenous in their interests, language, demands and aspirations either, at least not in cities.There will be ethnic and religious groups (some in open conflict), local political organizations vying for power, special interest groups (women, youth, disabled), people whose properties or interests border proposed new water lines, road improvements, wells or dump sites. There will be the union of small traders, the unemployed, the latest arrivals who have been displaced by the political conflict elsewhere or by the government's latest dam project. Very little will be known about their commitment to development in the face of their day-to-day need to survive and succeed.

Advising them all will be a body of consultants, some in private practice, many from academia. All will be engaged in some kind of search. Some academics will search for problems, for questions, for theories without much recourse to answers, asking 'why' without the need or will to get to 'what' or 'how'. It may work in practice, they will ask, but will it work in theory? They will be under pressure to publish their work in learned journals that will help them secure a place at the next international conference and that will earn their institutes more credence and cash in the next round of the government's grant allocations or equivalent. There will be fact collectors and serial thinkers, empiricists, rationalists and post-rationalists, positivists and neo-positivists, all skilled with their logical frameworks and research methodologies. Most will have lost their academic freedom long ago, in the competition for dwindling resources, in the insecurity of their jobs and in the progressive bureaucratization of academia.

As the competition for funds intensifies, so too does the demand for academics to distinguish their merits and expertise, as they compete with each other for survival. This search for distinction, geared as it must be to winning students, attracting research funds and influencing academic bureaucrats, is driven more and more by market-specific or client-specific criteria, rather than by subject-specific or need-specific criteria. The result is that academics adopt the institutional values and ambitions of governments, industry and international agencies that they subsume in their work and teaching. When there is innovation, it is driven by management not ideology – with indicators of performance, workload planning, role profile analysis and quality assurance criteria designed to ensure good ratings for the next round of grant awards. These bureaucratic pursuits bring with them a demand for entrepreneurship amongst staff. Those who before had maintained the high ground of academic debate – speaking the truth and exposing lies – have voluntarily or otherwise stepped down into the swamp of commercial enterprise and competition. Increasingly it is here that academic careers are decided. The result, despite the quality of research and consultancy still in evidence, is that even the most energetic find themselves paralysed by the sheer effort it takes to keep the system going.[19]

In contrast, and in practice, there will be others searching for answers without much recourse to questions or theory – the pragmatists who find it hard or undesirable to pass on their secrets to others because they have no time to stop and think, only to do, because of the competition for work. For them, theory is abstraction and gets in the way of practice. For consultants in private practice, time is short. They are in danger of what Popper called 'solutioneering': 'the jumping to solutions – reorganization, replanning – without spelling out what the problem was or if there was one'.[20] They are rational and pragmatic 'how-to, either/or' thinkers, attacking a problem if they do find one and inventing one if they don't. Their principal concern is, after all, to keep their business going. They will be looking to streamline, to find the shortest or least complex path to meeting their objectives, not giving too much away for fear that others may do it for themselves. Outputs (short term) will be more important than outcomes (long term), getting out of situations will be as important as getting into them.

Unravelling the strange structures of place, populated by all these actors in the interconnected settings and multiple agendas of city authority, national governments, global institutions, local activists and all the other vested and often competing interests, reveals a kind of rationale that is not easy to model and which practice often denies because it does not fit tidy routines or easily explainable relationships. For practitioners in these settings, the risk of surprise, of being wrong or ignorant, of making mistakes, admitting uncertainty, changing your mind or taking second place to non-professionals encourages a repertoire of defences – of more specialization and, at worst, more jargon and abstraction.

These responses exemplify old-paradigm thinking about the nature and purpose of development and practice.

In old-paradigm thinking, we held assumptions about development which guided our practice based on clear and unchallenged differentiations between *us* and *them*. The terminology of the day emphasized this division: first world and third world, developed and underdeveloped, developed and developing. Development, it was thought, could be engineered and brought to people by those who know best, in the form of technology, money and moral values that would make life better. It was something that was *done* to others, something that was *provided for* others who cannot provide for themselves. When we did occasionally invite people to provide for themselves, it was on terms agreed *outside*. Participation was a means to achieving pre-set goals, not an end in its own right. People followed the plans of planners; plans did not follow people.

Cause and effect was what old-paradigm thinking was about. It was directional, it was linear. Projects were short-term, predictable and finite. With sufficient resources (so it was thought) of technical assistance, technology and skill, with enough knowledge – enough, that is, to catch up but not enough to get too far ahead – then development could be achieved, and quickly. All of this was based on the belief that there was something wrong *out there* in the first place that needed fixing, that there was a problem which could be *solved* with a bit of help and money, so long as we all pulled together, so long as we all shared similar objectives, values and beliefs.[21]

When it came to poverty, economic growth would solve all. Its benefits would trickle down to those in most need, so we believed. And when it did not, we came to accept (or knew all along) that poverty was an integral part of growth and we built safety nets accordingly (subsidies, rebates, benefits and vouchers). In 1974, the UN called for a 'New International Economic Order' which would provide equity, sovereign equality, interdependence and cooperation.

In 1991, the UN tried again, adding 'human' to the term development in an attempt to shift the emphasis away from money and give development a spiritual boost. They called for choice, democracy, participation and freedom – social, economic and political. All of this was to reduce the gap between rich and poor, and to promote justice and peace, but which still has failed to arrive. The gap between rich and poor, nationally and internationally, got bigger, widened by, not bridged by, development – by the Washington Consensus, by the forces of globalization and neo-liberalism, by structural adjustment, deregulated markets, free trade tariffs and the rest:

> ... [T]he spectacular enrichment of the well-off fuels hopes of a possible redistribution among those left out in the cold. People cling on to their hopes all the more tightly in that some advance signs seem to be visible: some food surpluses have reached areas of chronic under-nourishment; or have enabled destitute authorities to pay their staff. A few billions of dollars, distributed each year by the rich countries as development assistance, finance publicly useful infrastructure, plug budget deficits, encourage the purchase of military hardware; NGOs mobilize civil society in the well-off countries ... in order to send gifts to the most disadvantaged sectors of the world population, to take financial responsibility for a clinic, to provide backing for cooperative ventures, to support educational institutions or credit provision... The essential thing is to keep the belief going.[22]

More so, the purpose of development assistance is to maintain the status quo and purposefully to ensure the gap between rich and poor is sustained. As long ago as 1908, Georg Simmel was pointing out:

> ... it becomes clear that the fact of taking away from the rich to give to the poor does not aim at equalizing the individual positions and is not, even in its orientation, directed at suppressing the social difficulties between rich and poor... The goal of Assistance is precisely to mitigate certain extreme manifestations of social differentiation so that the social structure (the current world order) may continue to be based on this differentiation.[23]

Today, we are less naïve about practical realities, we know differently. We have learnt the truth of opposites. We have learnt that development is ongoing, a process in which occasionally and from outside, some form of intervention is useful to open up opportunities, to facilitate access to resources, to act as a catalyst for change. There is no beginning and no end, no single measure of progress, no primacy given to any one set of values, at least not on paper. Human wellbeing is as important to economic growth as growth is to wellbeing. We find that trust and mutual respect now feature as criteria with which to judge the appropriateness of projects. Interdependence, not dependence, is what we seek, between people, organizations and between nations. New terms capture a new spirit, a new paradigm – rights, freedom, respect, civil society, sustainability and governance. Ethical considerations are paramount – the need to consider the harm we do as much as the good, conditioned by '...criteria for determining tolerable levels of human suffering in promoting social change'.[24]

All well and good in theory, but how far have we got in practice? We champion the cause of poverty elimination, environmental sustainability, rights and freedom and, at the same time, continue to praise growth and the benefits of global capital markets. 'The so-called global market', said Capra, 'strictly speaking is not a market at all but a network of machines programmed according to a single value – money-making for the sake of making money – to the exception of all other values... Money has become almost entirely independent of production and service... Capital (and economic power) is global whilst labour as a rule is local... Thus labour has become fragmented and disempowered'.[25] Castells, Capra, Chomsky and others conclude that, rather than alleviate or eliminate poverty, globalization and market fundamentalism perpetuate poverty and social exclusion, undermine local production in favour of imports, accentuate divisions in wealth between nations and within nations. Market fundamentalism undermines democracy because democracy, like environmental regulations, gets in the way of big business.

We promote good governance and, with it, partnership, interdependence, cooperation and decentralization, so giving a voice to civil society. And yet, governance, and in particular global governance, is not working. 'As the world becomes more globalized, our global institutions seem to have less and less legitimacy.'[26] Dependency and homogeneity are widespread and explicit objectives of the new global order, beneath all the rhetoric. Cooption not cooperation, material and cultural appropriation rather than integration are the orders of the day.

Politically, all nations will be under pressure to conform to a new world order driven by the forces of globalization and neo-liberalism, determined largely by the Washington Consensus (liberate trade, deregulate markets, zero inflation, privatize and eliminate government where possible) and decided by the G8 nations (USA, Germany, Japan, France, UK, Canada, Italy and Russia). Today the major initiative of international policy is the introduction of global integration into the agendas of global capitalism and neo-liberalism. 'All major powers', said Richard Haas, 'would be persuaded to sign on to certain key ideas as to how the world should operate... Support for free trade, democracy, markets. Integration is about locking them into those policies and then building institutions that lock them in even more'.[27]

Participation is championed by all and underpins governance and all the other millennium development goals. And yet, it remains largely token and largely instrumental; less to do with control, with empowerment or self-determination and more to do with 'tagging along' in the hope you won't be left out – politically and economically – when it comes to the distribution of aid. And, in planning, tyranny, not justice or empowerment, is systematic. Participation, it is argued, can override established structures, it normalizes radical engagement, coopts knowledge and empowers outsiders.

'While several countries have enacted progressive legislation regarding participation', concluded a report commissioned by the NGO CARE in five cities worldwide, 'in almost all cases, examples of real participation were hard to find. Fixed attitudes, low capacity and limited budgets within local authorities often leave participation as an add-on luxury rather than as a basic right or legal obligation'.[28]

Meanwhile, 940 million people continue to live in squalor, representing some 80 per cent of the urban population of the world's least developed countries.[29] And whilst the UN again put the blame firmly on the processes of globalization and neo-liberal economic policies, the development world continues to pontificate and theorize. Gilbert Rist gives us an apt summary. 'Development,' he says, 'has gradually been drained of content, so that it is now a mere residue used to justify the process of globalization'.[30]

Meanwhile, in the narrow and ramshackled streets of Kibera in Nairobi – the world's largest slum, housing some 600,000 people – or in Mumbai, Lima, Cairo and elsewhere, people organize, build homes, gain access to services and utilities in the inventive and enterprising ways they always did. It is here in this complicated and organic swamp of the everyday, with its adaptive and largely self-organizing systems of people and collectives who think locally and act locally, where the intelligence of cities lies, where small has long been difficult and even ugly, and where less is rarely perceived as more by those who have least.

PART 2
ENCOUNTERS IN PRACTICE

'On Balnibarbi, an island in the North Pacific, the citizens of Lagado, its capital city, are dressed in rags and rush through the streets with wild staring eyes. The poverty that reigns in Balnibarbi is largely the responsibility of the so-called Projectors. In about 1660, a group of people sailed to Laputa and returned after five months with a smattering of mathematics and their heads full of volatile spirits acquired in that lofty region. They immediately began to devise schemes or 'projects' for putting everything on a new footing. An Academy of Projectors was set up in Lagado: today every city of any consequence has its own academy. The 'projects' were designed to enable one man to do the work of ten, to produce buildings that never wear out, and to bring all plants and crops to maturity at any given time of the year. The difficulty is that none of these schemes has yet come to fruition and in the meantime the country lies in waste.'

Jonathan Swift, *Travels into Several Remote Nations of the World by Lemuel Gulliver*, 1726

It all started with a chance visit by the chairman of the National Housing and Development Authority to an annual seminar held at one of those prestigious academic institutions in the USA. The chairman was fishing for ideas of how to get his authority and his minister out of a fix. Recent statistics had shown an increasing demand for housing and services, if the government were to meet its pledge of adequate shelter for all. At the same time, there had been a demand by the IMF, following its recent visit, to cut subsidies and government expenditure by some 30 per cent, as a condition of its next round of lending. In any case, the recent spate of spending had made hardly a dent in the demand for shelter and had brought the housing authority close to bankruptcy.

At the seminar, the chairman listened to groups of academics championing the virtues of housing *by* people, of self-help, participation and enablement. 'Support people to provide for themselves', they said, 'rather than waste time and money providing for them'. He had come across these ideas before, in books and learned journals, but had dismissed them as radical. Now they offered him hope of political salvation. It was expediency, not ideology, which caught his attention.

Months later, he was to invite these same academics to explain themselves to his Minister of Housing who was also, as it happened, the Prime Minister.

The first visits of the expatriate team were, significantly, about changing the hearts and minds of ministers and bureaucrats in favour of what became known as a 'support-based approach' to housing and urban development. What did it mean? Whose authority would it threaten? What would it entail on the ground and how would it get started? At the Prime Minister's offices, in the prestigious architecture of the newly completed Houses of Parliament, we argued ideals not pragmatics: reawakening the spirit of community, building self-reliance, mobilizing the resources of ordinary people and giving voice to the silent majority.

In the months and years that followed, we worked with bureaucrats and managers, architects, engineers and others in city offices, community groups and NGOs, in cities and villages. We called the practical side of it 'Making Micro Plans' because we started small and because it was all about making and doing. With the help and motivation of entrepreneurial individuals with status and power in government positions, we set a new trend which would give substance to the enabling approach – en exemplar for theory and practice worldwide.

It all started in the highest of government offices, in the ivory towers of academia and in the minds of enlightened individuals – academics, practitioners and politicians. It began by cultivating first the right political climate for it all to happen on the ground, for liberating the latent potential of the everyday, and then by ensuring that what happened on the ground helped shape and redefine the politics and governance of city places.

2

DEPARTURES AND ARRIVALS

*How Nina lost her home and found a role, all with
the aid of Patama's little boxes.*

*Some men see things as they are and ask why. I dream things
that never were and ask, why not.*

Robert F Kennedy

Things as they are... things that never were... I first met Nina in
the lobby of a resort hotel – an unlikely but welcomed venue for
a seminar on the operation and maintenance of water supply. She
was there to present her latest achievement on the management of
solid waste. She had been an integral part of all the planning and
urban upgrading that had started under the new enabling policy
– a community builder and social entrepreneur. I visited her again
on one of those study visits I organize annually for my students so
that they could hear, first-hand, her story. Now, we sat down on her
crowded terrace as she recalled how they had won this new home
and with it, their dignity and independence.[1]

Nina is a short woman, colourfully dressed and self-assured
in that eager, inoffensive way so typical of her type; so different,
one notices, from the missionary zeal of her US and European
counterparts. Their compassion, she often found, was degrading
not comforting, their good intentions made matters worse because

they raised hopes and expectations in ways which could never be achieved. Nina's face bore none of the hallmarks of these zealots – their faces hard and pinched from years of arguing some worthy cause, dressed *down* to be one of them, recent arrivals, it always seemed, from some remote commune.

Nina talked without anger or resentment, despite years of social neglect and uncertainty about her rights, despite all the hardship and harassment that goes with being poor. She talked and smiled knowingly. Until recently, before her relocation to this new place in the old part of town, she had lived with her family of four children in one of those illegal canal-side settlements. She is one of those urban heroes who had been active for many years before her move: fighting eviction, negotiating rights to services and land, and later accepting the inevitability of relocation – turning it all to her advantage. She was a self-taught community leader, a self-qualified development practitioner. Her activist and advocacy skills and her powers as a negotiator had been learnt on the job. She had no career ambitions, other than to raise her standard of ordinariness and, with it, her dignity. She had trust enough in people, even government officials and those who had forced her to move, who she believed would always see reason to do things right and fairly, if only she and her like could get to them and explain their point of view and be reasonable themselves.

It was an early evening, she recalled, when the men from the housing department arrived. Their arrival was unannounced but unsurprising. It had happened before – more than once. The men gave notice to each householder – there were 76 families in total – that they were to leave and that this time it was for real. They had to be gone within 15 days. The land they had occupied for some 25 years had always been designated as public easement, designed to give access to vehicles to clean the canal and keep it in proper order. They told everyone that the government was getting tough on people who got in the way of city authorities doing their job. The canal was silted and polluted and the impact on health and hygiene was being felt citywide. They could either take the government's offer of compensation and move, or face the bulldozers. Some 64 families took compensation and went to squat elsewhere or moved in temporarily with family or friends. It became obvious that the remaining 12 families, on their own, were unlikely to succeed in their struggle for rights to stay, and that it was time to shift the emphasis of negotiation to their right to be resettled. Even then, the chance of success, given their numbers, was slim. Street talk soon connected them with a network of middle men and women who kept themselves informed about who was doing what and where and with whom with respect to housing, services and utilities. These people were themselves a loose network of wizened individuals and storytellers around the city, a collective whose tacit knowledge and gossip offered a valuable informal resource and service to communities about where to move, where to invade, which NGOs might help, who else to connect with, how best to argue their cause, how to dodge the authorities. These people serve as an observatory of the informal city, as talking notice boards, full of information and knowledge. They had formed themselves into a community network and set up an eviction hotline. 'The eviction hotline', we are told, 'is one of several ways the national, regional and citywide levels can rally resources and expertise to support individual communities and families when they need help. The hotline has proved to be not only an effective prevention but also a potent community network-builder. In the process of stopping eviction... the hotline has helped build national federations (of settlement communities) with enough clout to win the right to stay and develop their communities'.[2]

Studies in Mexico City and elsewhere have shown how this kind of social cooperation is one of the most important resources of the poor, a way in which the social risk of individuals is insured collectively. 'However we view the phenomenon of people organizing collectively... it is an important dimension of urban livelihood systems'.[3]

When agents like these, operating as they do, individually and informally coalesce and, through their network, act as a larger and single organization, when they are able to wield power and influence and become sophisticated, they emerge and become developmental.

In the weeks and months that followed, a new alliance emerged of some 43 families who were facing similar eviction threats elsewhere. With the help of an NGO and with advice from the hotline, they got organized and started a savings scheme in preparation for their move – a form of commitment to unity and cause that would also give them bargaining power. By the time they had found a place to move to, some three years on, they had accumulated sufficient savings for a down payment on land. As a cooperative, which now they were, they were able to secure a loan from the government housing department to finance the land and which left a little over for infrastructure, play equipment and landscaping. The NGO agreed to act as guarantor. A single title would be issued to the cooperative and the loan would be managed by the co-op's newly established management committee – set up and trained by their partner NGO. A private–private, private–public partnership emerged. For house building, families would need to find their own money, use their own resources. The days of free land and subsidies were over. Their first task, once formed, was to set up by-laws for the cooperative – a condition of continued membership and settlement on their new site: no drugs, for example, and no gambling; accept the concept of mutual care; no-one to put up a fence around their property; a good record of conduct, a commitment to self-management, particularly in looking after community facilities.

Nina's eviction and relocation is textbook stuff, typical of many but which reveals, at this early stage of our planning, a number of truisms, so difficult to quantify. Throughout, she reflected with pride how overnight they had shed their passivity and their dependence on landlords and city officials, and on a state system which fed on their cheap labour but which failed them when it came to housing and basic services.

And when they had housed themselves along the canal and had organized their own services, that same system had rendered them at once illegal and invisible. This lack of recognition had stripped them of their dignity. They had endured their state of not being, not because they had done wrong but because they were denied the right to do right, because they were poor in money and status, because they had always been – in the eyes of the officials – the problem. In the years of struggle, they had fought their way out of dependence through activism and alliance building, had won their independence and, with it, a sense of mutual respect, despite individual sacrifices. They had learnt to work as a collective, working their way out of exclusion and creating a new unity, a togetherness which met their common purpose, a community of interest which gave them power and worth. Nina's pragmatism, not idealism, won them recognition. Importantly, they learned to reframe their problems in ways they could tackle and which would give them status as partners rather than adversaries. At first, they had fought for the right to stay, but later argued their case for entitlement to safe and secure land, given their citizenship. This opened up new opportunities, connected them with other partners. Their emergence enabled them to join the mainstream and be ordinary.

At first, and on arrival at their new place, most felt vulnerable, despite their achievement. A new community: for most it would mean new jobs, new neighbours and new schools for children. They had, after all, lived in their old place for 25 years. They had transported what materials they could from their existing houses to build a starter home – advertising boards for walls, corrugated sheets, plastic, old doors, bamboo, rolls of linoleum for floors. Each had been allocated a lot of 6 × 14 metres, much smaller than they had before. And how did everyone decide which lot they got? 'We drew a lottery', she said. Later, people exchanged lot numbers to be near friends and family, to combine lots into family compounds, as they once had in their villages. Sometimes money changed hands to do so. I wondered whether we should care about this, given the coy way in which she offered her information, and then decided we shouldn't. Not everyone had moved at once. 'Some may never move here at all', she said. After five years, 20 plots were still vacant, used by settlers for growing vegetables. Their owners were probably living back in some illegal settlement downtown somewhere, waiting for the price of their land to go up before they would sell. And why not? Most of us who can, accumulate most of our wealth in property, usually our own – why deny this to the poor?

Over the years, most families had improved their houses, adding concrete or steel I-beam frames, tiles for roofs, a second floor. The road itself, at first compacted with earth, oiled occasionally to keep the dust down, now was concrete. Why pay the extra money for concrete? Because it looks good, like the good parts of the city – a place with status. And what of the planning process itself? How was the site laid out, how were lot sizes decided, houses designed, standards set?

A rooster interrupts our talk, a child cycles by on his homemade trike, the ice-cream lady plays her universally recognized jingle. We buy choc-ices. Kids stumble onto Nina's terrace. Nina attends to their questions and needs. We take our leave.

* * *

The following day we wanted to find out more about the planning process itself – in particular, what help families had received from their NGO and what lessons we could learn. I knew that Patama had been the architect to the group, working under the auspice of the Asian Coalition of Housing Rights (ACHR). She had been my student for a year in Oxford and was now an active community architect – an effective development practitioner. We visited her

Diagram A   *A stepped approach to getting what you need and want*

offices. She showed us a diagram she had used to introduce her community to the process (Diagram A). Its purpose was to get everyone thinking about the steps they would take and to put the brakes on rampant expectations. She wanted to dispel the idea that she was some fairy godmother, and that it would all happen by some wave of a magic wand tomorrow.

Patama tells her own story:[4]

> Early in 1996, I was asked to help the Santitham community to plan their housing design and construction. I first went to the community to talk to the people and get an idea about how they lived before, what they wanted and what kind of resources they had. I found the people very keen about planning their new settlement and houses, but unsure how to build on the 6 × 14 metre plots in the new land, which were much smaller than the roomy plots they rented at Santitham, which averaged around 200 square metres per family.
>
> In the early stages of the negotiation process, two standard house types were developed by a prominent architectural firm. Both designs looked good to me but, as might have been expected, the people wanted nothing to do with them and wanted to design their own houses. It is difficult to blame them. So I decided that the best I could do would be to find a way for the architects and the poor to meet somewhere in the middle and work on the designs together, each drawing on his/her own expertise and experience.
>
> We started the first sessions by getting to know each other and talking generally about the settlement. People are always shy [to start with] and so, to break the ice, we talked about all the difficulties of making shelter in the city for a family with very little money and no land. How did each family do it? How do people use their houses? What parts of the house were most important? What changes had they made over the years? I tried to connect all the subjects we talked about to concrete issues of space and function in their existing houses. Then I asked them to draw their own existing houses and add their comments about the space and functions. By this time, everyone had begun thinking about his/her house in terms of spaces and qualities which do or do not serve their daily lives. They had begun formulating ideas about what they wanted to keep or change in their new houses.

We started the second session by letting everyone draw a picture of his/her 'dream house' without worrying about budget or plot size. I found that despite this invitation to go wild, most people squeezed all their family's needs into houses that kept within the limits of extremely modest plot sizes and budgets. We pinned up all the dream houses on the wall. Most of them were very simple – not much more than three-dimensional descriptions of their most basic family needs. No castles, no palaces, and only two houses with tenuous suggestions of a swimming pool or a home-cinema! For me, this made clear that, for these people, even such a simple little house is already a 'dream'. I asked for some volunteers to explain their dream houses to the whole group, and let the others ask questions. The people all had fun giving each other critiques.

The next step was to make these 'dream houses' a little more real, given [all] the [usual] constraints. We gave everybody grid paper and scaled, cut-out furniture to stick on. We used the actual length and width of the community centre, where the workshops were held, as a life-size scale, to help people visualize the rooms they were designing at smaller scale. First, everyone drew the resettlement plot (6 × 14 metres) on the grid paper. Then they drew in their houses on this scaled plot, trying hard to squeeze in all the dream-house elements and ideas. After that, everybody made rough cardboard three-dimensional models from these plans. By now there was an element of friendly competition at work, and everybody was trying to make his/her model nicer than the others'.

When all the models were made, we laid out a big site plan (same scale as the models) on the floor and asked everyone to put his/her cardboard house on the plot. Suddenly, we all had a community in front of us. It looked awful, of course. Almost every house completely filled the little plot. There was no open space whatsoever, one roof drained onto another roof, no place for trees or air circulation. It was packed! When I asked the people whether they would like to live in this community, there was a chorus of unhesitating 'No's'. Then they started talking about how their new community should be. I did not have to tell them anything, no lectures about density or open space or setbacks. Everyone understood and agreed to leave a small amount of space open on each plot and then went back to readjust his/her house design accordingly. A set of site rules began to emerge.

In the next session, we divided people into groups according to family size and budget, so people with similar family sizes or budget constraints could borrow ideas from each other and help develop house designs together, more efficiently. But group members could not agree with each other's ideas, each one insisting his/her idea was the best. On top of that, the house-building budgets many of the people had been working from were much higher than their real affordability, since many were reluctant to reveal to the group the true extent of their poverty by stating such a low housing budget. This was a tricky problem but I was calm enough to ask them what we should do. At the end, the people gave us the idea of everyone somehow beginning from the 'same structure' but using it in different ways, according to 'different functions', which the people would manage by themselves.

Back in our office, we three architects sat down with the pile of designs from the people to find that common dimensional framework. The average size of the largest room was about 9 or 10 square metres, which could make a neat 3 × 3 metre module. This 3 × 3 metre module could also be conveniently built with and spanned by bamboo, which is cheap and widely available. So we made hundreds of small cardboard boxes, sized to scale, at 3 × 3 × 2.5 metres, each one representing a single structural unit.

Then using these 'building blocks', the people assembled another set of house models on their grid-paper plots. All the houses were completely different in area, orientation, mass and function. Some houses were small, some were big, some single-floor, some two-floor. Everyone was happy with this refinement of their house ideas and were able to explain their house models to the larger group. By this time we had, more or less, a set of preliminary house designs, based on this 3 × 3 metre module. Next we put the house models all together again, on the big site plan and saw how they all got along with each other. This time we could see much more open space, and could actually imagine living there. Everybody was satisfied with the sense of community that had been created.

Next, we showed everyone slides of some beautiful houses built in other countries with unconventional materials – bamboo, thatch, scrap wood and cloth. We gave everyone a simple table on which to list materials and quantities needed for his/her new house. First they had to see what materials they could salvage and reuse from their existing houses and then decide what new materials they would need, and how much those materials would cost. The people divided themselves into groups and went out into the city to gather information about the prices of various building materials. When everyone came back, we were able to put together a list of construction materials and their prices – some of which were very cheap.

Using plans drawn from the box models and a simple cost estimating sheet, the people then estimated their house costs. I did not have to persuade anyone to use the cheaper 'local' materials rather than the more costly steel and concrete. Some might first have wanted to use those concrete products which are symbolic of middle-class affluence but then they figured out themselves that using these materials would make their houses too expensive. One look at the cost of materials and families came to their own conclusions. This does not mean that we are against using concrete or steel, but considering the people's affordability and the hefty land-loan repayments they will have to make for many years, it makes sense to avoid deeper debt as much as possible. Gradually, houses can be upgraded as families can afford to do so.

The first house designed through this series of workshops was built in the first phase of the resettlement process. The owner is a woman who once claimed she knew nothing at all about housing design and construction, but the delightful house she built is filled with innovation, cost-cutting creativity and whimsy. She hired a couple of local carpenters to help her, and learned by doing. We came out to the site often and assisted as much as we could. She knew all the details and was able to deal with all problems on site. The overall cost of her house was low, working out to about 65 per cent of its market price. Later, when people asked me for details and cost figures about house designs on this settlement, I sent them to Nongyao and her neighbours – for advice!

In her new place, and a few doors down from Nongyao, Nina now lives in a small house of about 50 square metres, built with a small loan equivalent to about US$300 that she had secured from the government's new community credit bank, and which she had designed with the help of Patama Roonrakwit. She had used most of her loan to buy materials, windows and doorframes, a few ornamental balustrades to enclose her terrace, but mostly to construct a reinforced concrete frame, which she was now filling in, with the help of friends and family. She has a kitchen, proudly displaying a Happy Flame butane gas cooker, a small bathroom and a living room given status with the arrival of her new Toshiba refrigerator. At the back of the house there is an all-purpose room, full of enterprise. In one corner, newsprint is recycled into carrier bags for shopping. An old man, a friend of the family, sits weaving red and yellow plastic string into their tops to form handles. The rest of the room is given over to a sewing machine and piles of cured leather which enable her and her 18-year-old daughter to eke out a living making bible covers for the local bible society. Ever since her husband died some five years ago, her major sources of income are from money sent by another daughter who works overseas as a housemaid in one of the Gulf States, and from her home-based enterprises. In the middle of the house, concrete steps, roughly cast and unfinished, disappear to some unknown future through the roof slabs. Outside, back and front, there are pots, buckets, plywood, corrugated sheets, plastic sheeting, hosepipes, baskets, clothes lines, brooms, bits of scaffolding and scavenged ironware and dogs in kennels made of boxwood – nothing goes to waste.

There are now, in all, some 400 families living in this settlement, with weekly arrivals from other 'canal' communities, many of them engaged in the fishing business. The municipality, already stretched elsewhere, is unable to provide even the most basic of maintenance, not least to pick up the mountains of rubbish now dumped on any available patch of public land. The municipal area in which Nina lived, now a densely populated mix of formal and informal settlement, generated some 150 tonnes of solid waste each day, of which 100–120 tonnes were collected. Rampant and rapid urbanization had forced the authorities to dump what they had collected on environmentally sensitive land adjacent to a sanctuary of birds that were now under threat of extinction. As in any locality, the problems of waste were both local to residents and environmental for the city at large. There was, it seemed, mutual advantage for residents and authorities to get together and sort things out, but it all needed commitment and mediation.

3

THE COMPOSTING BIN: LOOKING FOR STARTERS

In which Mela spots the possibilities in a barrel of muck.

Nina's neighbour and longstanding friend is Mela,[5] another campaigner for community rights who had now turned her attention to improving conditions in the new settlement. During her days campaigning against eviction with Nina, she had got to know Seva[6] – an NGO actively in search of better ways of managing solid waste. Seva had long recognized that managing solid waste effectively involved reducing the amount generated for public disposal and ensuring that dispersal itself was profitable. Good solid waste management had as much to do with changing behaviour and habit as with organization and appropriate technical solutions – in particular, changing attitudes to realize that waste can be a resource, not something you throw away. The trouble is, that rubbish is rarely a priority for people locally, in the face of all their other problems and hardships. The ideological debate in favour of environmental conservation, consuming less energy and saving world resources – big issues indeed for national and global policy – holds little resonance for people struggling to survive on a daily basis. Nor does it score high on the political agenda of public officials – it's not a great vote catcher! But Mela's practical wisdom had already shown how self-interest, how a good measure of responsible selfishness, can bring about change and that most change starts best where it counts, on the ground, and with relatively quick pay-offs, if it is to be sustained.

Starting small, Seva had, for some time, promoted a composting bin – a 200 litre galvanized drum or barrel costing the equivalent of US$10, painted green to look good and worthy, and placed on a sand and cement base to keep it off the ground. They had calculated that something like 85 per cent of all waste generated in low- and middle-income settlements is biodegradable and that if they could convince people to use the composting bin, it would reduce considerably the amount of waste for disposal. Their tests showed how it took three months for the waste to decompose into compost, after which time it could be used on gardens or sold back to the municipality or to garden centres around the city. The non-biodegradable waste was then dumped in communal compounds for the usual weekly pick-ups.

At the same time, Seva, with Mela's cohort of composters, had organized meetings and events in schools and community centres to sensitize people to garbage and its associated problems of poor sanitation, to train women on how to segregate waste at source and compost the organic waste in barrels. Area clean-up programmes were organized, art and photographic exhibitions staged for youth on how to recycle materials – all part of an effort to get people interested and committed. Four months into the programme, there was an official event to launch the project by the city mayor, his inauguration helping to build a sense of pride in what could be a citywide initiative.

In the beginning, some 50 families agreed to pilot home-based sorting and composting, which increased over the first year to over 400, about half of the population of Mela's settlement. At first, things did not go so well, progress was slow. For one thing, the poorest people – those with the smallest plots of land – had little enough space to keep the bin, which required some 0.9 square metres and had to be somewhere near the kitchen. Nor did they have land enough to cultivate gardens, for which the compost would be useful. Waste for them was waste. In any case, the municipality were not to be trusted for weekly pick-ups. No markets for compost seemed to be available outside their own immediate area – no-one wanted their compost. Whilst the idea was popular amongst the more well-off and championed by conservationists and sponsors, for the poorer people the whole seemed more like a plot to get the municipality off the hook – to get the poor to do their jobs, like all the other participatory self-help projects they had heard about and seen. And so, whilst stories of success circulated amongst donors and academics who had visited as part of their research and who had written it all up in newssheets, research reports and journals, the rubbish continued to pile up wherever there was space available.

4

POWER POINTS, BULLET POINTS AND WASTE COLLECTORS: LEARNING FROM PRECEDENT

How Mela went abroad to talk about compost, learned some buzz words to help her know what she knew, and saw the limits of logic.

Meanwhile, Mela's reputation for community organizing won her a place on a study trip, organized by Seva and the UN Habitat Sustainable Cities Programme, to visit Bangkok with Nina. She had attended in the past a number of training programmes on gender and participation, community development and management, and leadership. She had enjoyed the status of those events, the people and contacts she had made but had found it difficult to connect the issues and processes talked about with her day-to-day problems. What she wanted to find this time were practical ways of sorting out rubbish and in ways that would profit everyone.

In Thailand, she visited a cooperative in Khonkaln set up to run a rubbish collection and recycling centre. Waste collectors buy into the cooperative which, apart from giving individual pickers a share in the profits of the whole, also gives them access to health care and guarantees a 'fair price' for materials. The centre provided information as to where there might be quality waste for pick-up and had developed clientele in schools, markets and in municipal buildings. In the early days, they had run at a deficit but now were turning profits equivalent to some US$400 a month. These profits were being ploughed back into the business. The cooperative was proposing to buy their own machines to process recyclable materials and had begun the task of setting up a network of sub-centres around the city for collecting and sorting. As for the municipality, they were advertising the success of the centre, exploring markets for material and issuing community contracts for solid waste management in other communities. Strong organization, leadership, small loans enterprise partnerships with pickers and municipality had launched this impressive network, had served to improve the lives and working conditions of individual pickers, and was cleaning up the city in environmentally friendly ways.

In an example from The Philippines, at Payatas, the Payatas Scavengers Association had set up a recycling resources centre – a place to explore the different ways in which materials and waste could be turned into marketable products. In this example, one could observe all around 'kids on skateboards made from hubcaps, chickens inside fences made from mattress springs, and men playing checkers with bottle caps. In home-based workshops people made scrubbers from fishnets, doormats from cloth scraps and dustpans from cookie tins'. The centre had secured some 2 hectares of land from the church and was carefully working out what best to do cooperatively and what to leave to individuals.[7]

During the visit, Mela, Seva and the rest of us attended two days of presentations and workshops with other members of community-based organizations, NGOs, officials from the planning authority and academics. It was organized in a resort hotel and golf club, some distance from the city, where participants could stay and work undisturbed by daily routine. It was one of those dissemination events required by donors – a 'sharing of knowledge and experience session' with some 40 attendees. It was all a relief from the mud and squalor of all those places we had visited so far.

The first speaker, a self-assured academic speaking on behalf of his World Bank sponsors, set out the larger picture. He was there to make sure that when it came to talking of waste, water, shelter or health, they would all feature in the context of the bigger themes of the day – good governance, livelihoods, rights and sustainability – words that caption key themes but which often hide as much as they reveal. He spoke with some detachment, a way of coping with the limits of his own (local) knowledge without losing belief in himself, without sacrificing his status and esteem internationally. He had become skilled at turning his ignorance to advantage and subscribed to Heisenberg's Uncertainty Principle (Heisenberg's Uncertainty Principle: the impossibility of knowing everything about a situation). Not knowing, he knew from his readings of quantum science 'leaves space to think creatively... uncertainty gives room to think'. It changes fundamentally power relationships because it invites questions, the answers to which are not already pre-set. In this sense, not knowing encourages the participation of others to engage with each other in search of ideas not based on pre-established routines, nor on so-called best practices.

Our pacesetter speaker was an outsider, an academic bound to draw best principles from good practice, to make professional sense out of common sense. His business was to articulate the tacit knowledge of all the Mela's in this world who knew much more than they could speak about, and pass it on to others through books, journals, manuals, guidebooks and talk shows. His political savvy and entrepreneurship, picked up over the years working with political leaders and community leaders, World Bank, UN and other agency staff, with NGOs North and South, with private corporations and government agencies, with fellow academics, practitioners, charities, world-savers and doom-mongers, had taught him the art of convergence and trust building as a prelude to productive discussion and plan making, which he was to endure after his talk. His presentation, in this sense, was a form of ritual exchange, a performance designed to build trust and association amongst his audience, to turn a collective of separate individuals into a society of development practitioners, even more than to convey knowledge and experience. His bigger task was to enable his audience to find themselves in what he was saying, to be inclusive of people's ideas and beliefs and tolerant of their prejudices without compromising his own convictions. During discussions, he knew how to say 'yes and' rather than 'yes but', recognizing the value of knowledge and experience of those who may be unequal, respecting the views of those whose interests may lead them to disagree and yet are able to work together. He offered 'impulses and guiding principles' rather than strict instructions, working initially without set rules, without set goals. This is the art of facilitation which Kaplan refers to in his book, *The Development Practitioner's Handbook*. In it, he says 'development facilitation as a professional discipline is an art rather than a science. For there are no rules, no regulations, no linear sequences of cause and effect, no real predictability. We cannot know whether a chosen intervention was the correct choice or not until we have actually made the intervention and observed the results'.[8]

During the early and formal part of the presentation, Mela was muddled by the jargon and acronyms familiar to others and confused by all the diagrams of bubbles and squares and arrows, which she chose to ignore. She was more entranced by the speaker's ability to conjure up images from nowhere onto the screen using his computer. It reminded her of all the magic shows she used to attend as a child at street carnivals in her village and soon found herself enjoying this show precisely because of its sophistication and intrigue. She felt in good company. She was getting over her awkwardness. When it came to good governance and sustainable urban management, the academic talked of the importance of partnerships between the state at the local level, civil society and the private sector. Something he said about bringing back the state as an enabler and to provide enabling frameworks that were transparent and accessible 'with competent bureaucracies that have adequate capacities for resource management and policy making and implementation'.[9] Fairness, inclusiveness, citizen respect for state institutions, protection of human rights, fighting corruption, promoting information flow were all key themes in his presentation. He went on to quote the Habitat Agenda for Good Governance:[10] decentralization of responsibilities; participation of civil society; partnerships; capacity building of all sectors; networking amongst organizations; and information to support sustainable urban development. Fine words, Mela thought, which lacked the feel and smell of the real thing, made a pleasant noise but had no meaning for her. Worthy, Mela was sure, but boring and wishful thinking, in her country at least.

The speaker reasoned it all in three ways: the failure of the state to provide (no argument there, she thought); the forces of globalization and notably the restructuring of the global economy (she had no idea what he meant); the greater social activism and importance of community and their NGO partners who were today delivering and managing a whole variety of goods, services and utilities, and increasingly taking a stand on basic rights. Mela began to link what he was saying with her own place and experience.

It confirmed her status and gave recognition to her and all the others in the room who were doing all these things. That she and her colleagues could, in their own way with their small struggles and success on the ground, contribute to what others called good governance and sustainable urban development resonated well with them, made them feel good, made them feel important and part of something much bigger than their own place. These outsiders, she thought, had the capacity to take a 'thing' – a composting bin, a standpipe, a community centre – and turn it into a big idea. She and her colleagues were part of their inspiration. Whilst at first she had been resentful of all the jargon and its abstraction, she now felt empowered by it. The stories he told, the examples he gave, the procedures he set out showed how their activism was an important part of development, not something peripheral to it. They were the mainstream. Mela was a development practitioner and not just a community worker, as she was called at home. She wondered what people would think of her new-found status when she got home. She imagined them cheering her on and voting her their next president.

That evening, she drew her own diagram to try to make practical sense of what she had seen and heard and which she would present to her community on her return. Modelled on the presentation she had seen and liked during the planning of the site after eviction, it showed a series of steps, with step one starting out with composting bins as they had done already back home, working her way up step by step toward a clean and healthy neighbourhood. Then she changed her mind. The effort that she and others had put into convincing people to compost their waste had few and tangible benefits for families, not least in the short term. What they needed was a first step that would clearly lead to profit for all.

She recalled one participant who, when asked what she thought governance meant, had responded, 'Clearing rubbish or putting in water, or managing health in ways that profit everyone, and fairly'. On her ladder, she placed on the first step recycling, followed by income, then marketing, employment, and clean and healthy neighbourhood. Their ultimate goal: to be rich with inner income – with status, dignity and self-respect as much as with money and things. Each step would be helped by people and organizations that would be partners, some with duties, others – government officials – with obligations. It was the grass roots equivalent of a logical framework, a business plan with activities, risks, outputs and indicators of achievement which they would work at collectively, not something passed down by donors. She would present it for discussion to her working group the next day but she was shy of its simplicity and its naïve-looking graphics. How impressive it would be, she thought, if she could magic it all on the screen just like the first speaker.

The following day we listened to one of the local NGOs (one of us, an insider) present a case study – a best practice example of a sanitation programme planned, implemented and managed by the community. The speaker admitted there was little or nothing new or innovative about the project itself but there was something to learn from all the social and organizational preparation before the project got started. His advice to CBOs was common sense and good. See what resources you've got inside before you go begging outside; keep your organization small to start with and don't worry that those who may get involved first are the motivated and elite who will have a strong self-interest, people you may not even like or trust; provide training where necessary and in particular to help progressively adapt traditional knowledge and wisdom to the non-traditional settings that may have been triggered by conflict, natural disaster or by the process of urbanization; accept that all these processes develop progressively – they are not one-off events delivering instant results, they take time and commitment and will involve all kinds of people, not all of whom are on your side, nor share your ideals.

It was a rebel rousing and impassioned call for a reawakening of the poor, more a sermon than a speech. He talked throughout by way of example, placing himself on the platform as a role model: do it like us and you can all become like us. As we watched his display of slides and his confident, sometimes arrogant, manner, Mela and her colleagues felt envy for all their achievements and their newly found status of best in this international forum. His community had transformed their place and lives. It all looked clean and good and lively. And yet his compassion was patronizing and his manner instructional. His desire to win us to their ways was boastful more than inspiring and placed him apart from his colleagues. He was surprisingly disempowering because he made Mela feel inferior, which is a barrier to taking action on your own, and because she felt guilt for not having done more or achieved as much. In their draft report *Enhancing Access to Human Rights*, the International Council on Human Rights cites guilt as one of the psychosocial barriers to achieving rights.[11] 'Guilt and oppression', they say, 'result in further alienation from mainstream institutions and can lead to low self-esteem and depression, inhibiting energy at both a personal and collective level'. On reflection, and later in discussion, two issues emerged from his presentation which placed him in contrast to the first speaker. First, the classification of 'best'; and second, and because of it, the feeling of envy, which 'has the power to suspend [our] judgement of reality'.[12]

'Best' means most excellent, most suitable, most desirable, something which surpasses all others. It is an ultimate state beyond which there can be little improvement, at least for now. It differentiates between talents hierarchically, and therefore unequally, and assumes single standards. It normalizes ambition and desires, differences in need and ideas from place to place, people to people. And, because it inspires envy, it undermines the self-respect of ordinary people. According to Sennet, 'self-respect fades when we respond to the example set by others'. In this sense, he quotes from Rousseau's *The Discourse on the Origin of Inequality*:

> *He who sings or dances the best, he who is the most handsome, the strongest, and most adroit or the most elegant becomes the most highly regarded; and this is the first step towards inequality, and at the same time towards vice.*[13]

The desire to become someone else, to join those whom society's institutions have deemed best, invokes envy. 'Modern society', says Sennet, 'invites us to envy; in a world bent on destroying tradition and inherited place, on affirming the possibility of making something of ourselves through our own merits, what keeps us from becoming another person? All we have to do is imitate the sort of person we would like to be'. But if we take up this invitation, Sennet points out, 'we find ourselves participating in our own loss of self-respect and subsequently in our own underdevelopment'.[14] We acknowledge our inferiority. We become poor in status and not just in money. We participate as inferiors in projects and programmes designed by others, trusting their will and intent because, by doing so, we may just get something which, after all, is better than nothing. And once we are seduced by their routines, by their logic of cause and effect, by their brand of best, we find ourselves admitting that our own ways, our traditional wisdoms, habits and even belief systems are second best. Our sense of inferiority is confirmed and we become vulnerable to manipulation. This takes many forms – through market forces, participatory programmes and capacity building. Mela and her colleagues had, time and again, subscribed to having their capacities strengthened by others so that they could better copy others and be mainstreamed. Capacity building, like the old-style planning consultations, became a form of cooption rather than a means to self-development. Whilst you may well acquire new skills and regain some sense of dignity and respect as a result, you do not acquire the capacity to become interdependent nor that broader awareness of your options, which helps you decide the best course of action.

The following day, our last before returning, the visitors were taken to visit the city's planning department to get an overview of their work and projects. Their offices were housed on the upper two floors of a five-storey concrete-frame building. The lifts were no longer working and the stairs were crammed with people waiting to get permissions of one kind or another, others selling soft drinks or cigarettes and yet others enjoying their afternoon siesta on landings in the coolness of the building. Jostling between them all were the office clerks and janitors responding to urgent calls for coffee and paper, keeping the flow of both circulating in equal measure.

We were shown into a large room with chairs in rows with a big mahogany-style table in front, on it a flower pot, water and two glasses – all in preparation for the speech that was to be made by the deputy city planner. On the walls of the room, at the back, an exhibition of maps and photos. Taking pride of place, a colour Master Plan of circles and arrows with patterns of green, grey and red, all fading a bit, denoting areas zoned for play, recreation, new housing, industry and the rest. It painted a world that was utterly in contrast to what we had observed days before. It was described according to some plan that views the world as discrete functional bits separated into tidy manageable zones, to a backdrop of posters and photos of Brasilia, Chandigahr or Milton Keynes. The terms used were abstractions of reality picked up, no doubt, in planning schools of the 1960s: 'magnets to attract circulation', 'communication nodes' instead of bus stops, 'lines of pedestrian communication' instead of walkways. Other plans and photos showed the latest in the government's low-income social housing schemes of three-storey walk-ups, all with donor support. All around, photos of happy residents and people who had been consulted, mostly standing in groups applauding their local MP and, with him, the chief planning officer who had made it all possible and who was predicted to be the next city mayor. Other displays boasted the latest city initiatives in slum upgrading – the new latrines, the standpipes, the paved walkways, the new school and community centre. In big letters beneath a photo of this new building we read 'Building Community – Building A New Future'.

All of this comes at a time when that old paradigm, based on Newtonian thinking – which is deterministic and reductive and which values certainty and predictability, trying hopelessly to pin it all down – is today displaced in favour of emergence, self-organization and holistic thinking. Holistic thinking moves us away from certainty and instead, toward an appreciation of pluralism, an acceptance of ambiguity and paradox.[15] As I wandered about the exhibit in the half-hour or so before the presentation, I reflected on my own training as an architect, encouraged as I was to find order to all the complexity and mess we encounter every day and give this expression in plans and buildings, to make it all certain and to be in control. We were schooled to take as precedent the old masters – just as my senior colleagues here were doing – those architects and planners whose plans and schemes were singular in their understanding of domesticity, of family, work and community. These they argued to be collective things that can be arranged and rearranged, rather than collective actions – something homogenous that you can point to, predict and model. All this they enshrined into buildings and master plans. In this way, it was easy to reduce the complexity of commerce and work into office parks, business centres, shopping malls and industrial estates; healthy play becomes playgrounds, recreation centres and theme parks; housing becomes lowest-common-denominator houses. Built into these plans were radical and unscrupulous shifts in power structure – a redrawn map of territorial and political control, an implicit transfer from private to public, from bottom to top, from small units of organization to large ones, from informal systems and emergent networks to ones that are formal, designed and tightly controlled, all 'achieved at the expense of lost potential'.[16] Chandigahr, Unite, Brasilia, Broadacre: the garden cities were masterpieces of planning and architecture, serving society by reforming it – defining a new era of city development and based on some absolute truth decided by its designers. Le Corbusier, for example, the master of them all, 'always assumed that his architecture was a response to the great new era; and indeed its magnificent new forms derived their élan from his conviction that they were part of a still greater transformation. When the revolution he expected did not occur, he did not abandon his architecture. He ignored the social context and created isolated monuments to his own genius',[17] much as we were taught to do in architecture school and much as students are still taught today.

The problem with these thinkers was not that they had a totalizing vision or subscribed to master narratives or indulged in master planning. Their problem was not that they had conceptions of the city of the social process as a whole. Their problem was that they took the notion of thing and gave it power over the process. Their second flaw was that they did much the same with community. Much of ideology that came out of Geddes and Howard was precisely about the construction of community, in particular about the construction of communities that were fixed and had certain qualities with respect to class and gender relations. Once again the domination of things seemed to be the general flaw...[18]

Our speaker confirmed the prevalence of old-paradigm thinking which underpinned his exhibits and his government's plans, despite all the development rhetoric. Mela had taken a seat way at the back. She told me later how she was uncomfortable but strangely excited by the setting. The only time she had been in a planning office before was as an activist fighting the authority over her eviction and then only after intimidating the guards with bared breasts and forcing her way in. She worried about her progressive conformity to people and organizations she had fought for years. She comforted herself with an old saying that came to mind and which went something like 'if you want to cross the river you have to learn to swim with the alligators'.

The speaker was one of those self-assured planners who wallow in statistics; a 'serial thinker' – someone who relies heavily on his intellect, who is good at solving problems and achieving tasks. For those people, B always follows A in the same way. They are goal-oriented or instrumental 'how-to' thinkers. They are rational and logical: if I do this then I know that a certain consequence will follow. Their thinking is linear and intolerant of nuance or ambiguity. Unlike associative or quantum thinking – the heart and spirit of the mind – serial thinking is strictly one-off, 'either/or' thinking and, whilst it may be fast, precise and even reliable, it is also inflexible, says Zohar. All three kinds of thinking are necessary to our understanding of complex systems, not least urban ones. But practice, and especially development practice, demands a lion's measure of the heart and spirit. Network governance, emergence, self-organization and much of the action science method which underpin good practice today draw substantially on the heart and spirit of the brain and on that ability to feel your way through and improvise, to change direction when needed without compromise.

This is all in stark contrast to our serial thinker who, by now, was busy putting his evidence into categories according to statistical circumstances which had led the government to its current policies on housing, health, education and the rest. There were income percentages, satisfaction levels, employment characteristics, household compositions, mobility patterns, gender ratios, child mortality rates, literacy rates, truancy rates derived from endless and costly surveys diagrammed on bar charts, pie charts and graphs, all justifying one way or another his urban policies, his plans and programmes. His was the kind of logic that categorizes everything: things and ideas became mutually exclusive.

As our own speaker talked on, it became evident that his presentation could have been made anywhere and to anyone. His audience was mere expediency – they were his statistical resource. He said a lot but, for Mela at least, explained very little. He was boring. Towards the end, he summarized using the ubiquitous overhead projector and a series of transparencies with justified bullet points. He had the habit of hiding the next bullet point. In her boredom, Mela found herself guessing what he might reveal next – perhaps a minister's name in the latest scandal, a tip for the horse races, a special offer on ladies' handbags. Her thoughts wandered back to her resort hotel, to the expansive pool with its uniformed attendants, the manicured lawns and Copacabana-type poolside bars with people on stools sipping whatever, in their scanty swimming costumes. She couldn't imagine their world but had seen them in magazines and in those advertisements outside travel agents, at beach resorts close to her home. She dreamt things that she knew could never be...

5

NEEDS AND RIGHTS: SOME FORMAL PLANNING

A process gets underway. And because you have to start somewhere,
we start by looking for a place to start.

Back home, the planning process began in earnest. At the planning workshop, Mela talked of her learning in Bangkok. She presented her stepped diagram for enterprise and waste recycling, which she never did have a chance to discuss in Bangkok. She talked of the need for strong organization and leadership, an alliance or network of small organizations, each with their own specific and local agendas around the city, but together offering an approach to build social as well as financial capital. She talked of partnerships with public authorities and with private-sector manufacturers of paper, plastics and other materials. There was the importance of profit sharing, of expanding markets to schools, of information on where to pick up what materials and where the demand may be for those materials. She gave examples of how their organization might give access to welfare, like the one in Pataya, and may offer training and other awareness programmes on health and home-based industries related to waste; of the need for a recycling resource centre on how to turn waste into marketable products; how land for such a recycling centre was needed and how maybe to negotiate formal contracts with the local authority in order to move on from volunteering – a community contract, maybe.

Most important, she came back with words and ideas which would enable them all to connect what they wanted on the ground with what the government authorities needed for their large, longer-term developmental goals of good governance, sustainability and effective urban management. She had learnt in Bangkok that it all had to be mutual – that there had to be give and take, that it had to be based on the need to work together rather than having to worry about good guys and bad guys and whose side you were on.

She talked as someone who had regained her dignity and worth. And as she talked, I recalled again the writings of Sennet and the three forces which he says challenge mutual respect: unequal ability, adult dependency and degrading forms of compassion. 'Respect', says Sennet, 'is fundamental to our experience of social relations and self'. It is an integral part of our social development. I came to realize that throughout Mela's descriptive assessment of her learning, which was based on urgent need and her achievements so far, was the underlying desire to be heard and seen and to be recognized. She sought to build her dignity, her 'inner capital' and that of her community and wanted no favours. But they did want recognition, which they knew they could not take for granted. Their potential to achieve was capped by their class and status. 'Self-respect', says Sennet, 'comes when difficulties are mastered, not when something comes easily. And mutual respect develops when we give recognition to someone else who may be doing or thinking something different' but still working in unison as an ensemble, as they were learning to do with municipal authorities and private companies. Development happens, I thought, when you succeed in the face of adversity, however small or limited the first steps may be. In this way Mela, and the many thousands of urban heroes like her, had earned their reputation as servant leaders.

In this phase of formal planning, and in a workshop, Seva and those of us ex-patriots and local academics who were assisting, sought to identify needs and rights. We looked for linkages between seemingly discrete and sometimes hidden systems and organizations, to connect more of the system to itself, to strengthen the alliances and build networks and to make sure it would all be sustainable. We needed to move on, for example, from composting bins and begin a series of parallel processes that would turn needs into assets. Later we would turn our attention to issues of rights as a way of prioritizing needs and work out ways in which rights can be made integral to planning and practical action.

The planning workshop entailed both various parallel sessions and other sessions at different times and on different days so that those who might otherwise have been excluded or intimidated (children, women or minorities) could be involved. In these other sessions we solicited the needs and priorities of those who may not have had a dominant voice. In one example, we asked children to tell their experience of what happened last time the area flooded. It was a session in a local school facilitated by Oliver Hamdi and Tara Franks. Diagrams, drawings and words told of displacement, loss of school time and time with friends, loss of possessions and snake bites. Women working in a parallel session added another view: loss of income, no fresh water, no access to shops, damage to property, fear for children.

In all cases, we triangulate the needs and priorities of as many stakeholders as possible, as a prelude to formal planning.

The planning process we practise is grounded in Action Science and follows the well-tried Community Action Planning[19] routine:

- assess problems and opportunities
- set goals and priorities
- identify options and trade-offs
- establish resources and constraints
- form project teams and tasks

The process begins with identifying problems – in a manner that avoids apportioning blame – and with identifying opportunities. Problem-solving will depend on problem-finding. 'It is through repeated social articulation of the problem which defines its spatial location and extent, rather than arrived at through a series of analytical planning studies'.[20] The initial list of wants might be favourite laments of individuals (we must stop squatters) or slogans of politicians (provide water for all). It is also likely that problems which may be high on the planners' agenda have no resonance at the institutional or political level (increased coordination, lower standards, preservation of aquifers). Yet sieving out individual problems or clusters of problems which are widely held and strongly believed to be solvable within a foreseeable future is the crucial starting point for action planning, 'establishing the initial condition for pursuing legitimate objectives for planning'.[21]

Analysis at this stage will focus on clarity, with four objectives in mind: to avoid preconceptions about solutions that will come to mind as problems are discussed (for example, our children need more facilities for play, why can't we have a new playground?); to observe where there is already consensus about issues; to flag potentially conflicting demands; and to read what seem to be differences but are in fact similarities expressed or interpreted in different ways. In all, the need is to position problems well enough in order to open avenues and explore solutions.

The progressive definition of problems, prioritized, interpreted and positioned according to cause and effect (why is it a problem and to whom?), is a basis for goal setting – what do we as stakeholders need? What resources do we have? What can we realistically build on? What can we realistically expect to achieve? Goals are prioritized according to need and then ranked according to feasibility. For each option we devise, we give some consideration to the risks involved, the investment entailed, the commitment demanded and the likely constraints to be encountered. How likely is it that we will get what we want if we ask for a new school building and what or who is likely to get in our way? Should we modify this demand? How much money will it entail and what investment of time and energy? To what extent will it tie us down over the longer term in repayments, tasks, time and so on? Constraints are analysed in terms of what of will get in the way of getting projects going, which will typically include institutional, financial, technical, environmental or political hurdles that have to be overcome. Once identified, ideas and procedures for overcoming hurdles are brainstormed – who can help, how and when? Do-able projects are identified – those that can start sooner rather than later – and then analysed in terms of their resource demands and their relative dependencies and interdependency.

During the final phase of this initial process, project teams are formed and a plan of action is devised to jump-start it all. 'Whilst these projects may be ill-conceived, uncoordinated, technically naïve, fragmented, socially unproductive (just to list a few of the common criticisms advanced from the armchair of analytical planning), they represent developmental avenues behind which the desire (and a degree of competence) to implement is manifested'.[22]

The list of needs that emerges from this initial exercise is familiar and typically long: security of land tenure, more jobs, transportation to markets, clean and adequate supply of water, better fire-fighting arrangements, mitigate the damage caused by floods and a sports facility for the children. Some call for better security, for more streetlights, safe ways of crossing roads, a better sense of place and community. Other needs are flagged by the municipal authority who, consistent with international trends and keen to please their donors, is working with its NGO partner on good governance. They seek to meet the needs of people through partnership with private-sector organizations and community groups. Malnutrition, particularly among young children, social inclusion, gender equality and rights are their agenda of needs.

We recognize, however, that not all of the needs can be met and look to prioritize the list. In any case, we ask: most who live in the slums and informal settlements of cities everywhere, to some extent suffer similar conditions and have similar needs, but are these needs a risk to life or to livelihood? Does the flood interrupt work, destroy houses, bring down power lines, interrupt school for more than a day or so, contaminate drinking water and spread disease? And then what priority, given our limited resources, do we invest in strengthening the structure of houses to prevent damage or collapse, or look to ways of preventing the flood water reaching houses, or a bit of both? Or do we raise the height of the plinth and accept that for two or three weeks a year (rather than four or five) there will be a risk of water in houses?

In this next phase of planning, we turn our attention to these questions, to risk and safety as a way of positioning need and, in particular, to the right to safety that is implicit in the International Agreement on Human Rights. The right to safety is implied in the Universal Declaration of Human Rights, the International Covenant on Civil and Political Rights and, in particular, in the International Covenant on Economic, Social and Cultural Rights.

Together, these documents offer us a framework on which to hang the right to safety as an explicit objective of urban development and integral to the planning process. This framework already includes 'the right to the highest attainable standard of health, to adequate food, shelter, safe water and sanitation, safe and healthy work conditions and safe environmental conditions'. Whilst the perception of risk is often relative and subjective, the term 'highest attainable standard' holds good intent and recognizes relativity.[23]

We group our assessment of risk into four categories: (1) risk from natural disaster (in our case, flood); (2) risk from social or political conflict or exclusion (in our case, class and caste differences, land security, employment and education); (3) risk from everyday hazards (water, sanitation, food or fire); and (4) risk from lack of resources or opportunities (transportation, information, education and employment). Many of the categories overlap. Many of the issues are interrelated. But it helps us to articulate needs – it gets us going and engages the discussion on risk reduction. There are seven steps in this process:[24]

1. assess risks
2. decide interventions
3. evaluate constraints
4. decide partners
5. anticipate harm
6. evaluate livelihood security
7. agree obligations

We start our risk assessment with identifying all the needs in our first phase of planning – floods, fire, water and the rest, grouped initially into our four risk categories. We ask what are the risks and where and how they impact livelihoods or wellbeing. We want, at this stage, to identify not only the effect (in the case of floods, for example, damaged houses, snake bites, polluted water) but the cause (poor standards, inadequate maintenance, wrongly located wells, no water storage facilities at home, lack of advance warning, lack of knowledge or information).

Next, we brainstorm the different ways we mitigate risk and, for each, the advantages or disadvantages and their trade-offs –

technical, financial, institutional, environmental and so on. This agenda of intervention will be complementary to those identified during the needs assessment done earlier (security of land tenure, jobs, better transportation, clean water, better fire-fighting equipment). It helps validate or invalidate earlier ideas and may identify other partners as integral to planning and implementation or management. If we take, for example, the contaminated drinking water, we might consider a community-level emergency water supply, or household-level water purification, or relocating tube wells and open wells. For each, there will be cost implications and also implications for management and maintenance. Overall, there will be a range of low-cost measures to control floods and mitigate risks. These measures might include better drainage; small bridges to give access to schools, shops, clinics where otherwise access will be interrupted; or the planting of shrubs and trees to stabilize embankments and prevent erosion. Equally, one might opt for building a local capacity 'in community' – a community disaster-management committee whose job it might be to assess risk, open lines of communication between people and with the authorities, raise awareness on health, contamination, preparedness issues, lobby the authorities on risk reduction measures and deliver first aid.

Just as with the needs-based approach, there will be constraints to implementing each of these ideas and interventions. Some will be technical, some will be legislative; others may be financial and yet others organizational. In this third phase of our planning, we seek to evaluate the constraints with a view to adapting, changing or even removing standards or legislation that get in the way of achieving objectives. We need to ask what, why and for whom these constraints exist. After years of floods, why is there still little or no community initiative or organization for mitigating risk? Why is there a lack of strong leadership in this respect? Is there adequate technical help, enough information? Are building codes adequate? Are they enforceable? Do the criteria for locating water facilities include the incidence of flood? Does government care that much? Is there the political will to help, given that the site of the most serious flooding is illegally settled and has been for 20 years? Why is there a perception amongst locals that flood prevention is a government job demanding major intervention, well beyond their local means? Why do people lack confidence in their own abilities to solve problems?

By now, we have a sense of who might be involved in each of the areas needing attention. We identify more specifically who these partners are, according to the state, the market and the community. We agree roles and responsibilities and assess potential areas of conflict of interest by doing a stakeholder analysis.

In all work, however worthy the intent, someone or some group is likely to come out less well off than others. Some may even be disadvantaged, as we will see later in our 'search for community' and the building of a community centre. In the same way, with the introduction of formal infrastructure, informal service providers may lose out and social capital may be lost. In this fifth phase of work, therefore, we try to anticipate harm so that it can be minimized or safety nets can be designed. We anticipate harm in respect to the household, the community in question and the larger urban society. In respect to our interventions, we ask: will the extra resources devoted to the flood-prone part of the settlement serve to empower that area at the expense of others and, in so doing, create further social division? Will the existing leadership be threatened by new leadership structures – those who will run the new savings organization or the community disaster-management committee? Will all the effort to self-manage and organize, to contribute your labour to all this work, pay less than other work? Will it undermine your livelihood? And, if some people contribute more than others, is there likely to be resentment and more division?

In the sixth phase of work, and in recognition that whatever interventions we make to solve practical and 'now' problems to reduce 'now' risks, in the long term these interventions must also contribute to building household livelihood security. We anticipate, as far as we can at this stage, how all the various initiatives which have been decided upon will help build assets – social, financial, physical, human resource and political. Not all will contribute to all categories. But, with each intervention, we attempt to multiply the benefits and achieve the widest possible impact. How much social capital has accrued from any community organization, or human resource capital from all the training in risk reduction, and from all the knowledge and information? How does all the new infrastructure contribute to the community's physical assets? And what about the dignity, respect and self-esteem that emerge from all these achievements? Has the capacity to lobby government and get what you need been enhanced as a result of all the training or organizing?

Finally, we decide obligations amongst stakeholders – a kind of social contract or commitment to the right to safety: to *respect* a right by avoiding action that may hinder or prevent its implementation; to *protect* the right to safety against those who might threaten it; to *fulfil* these obligations by taking agreed steps towards their realization.

From this early and cyclical analysis of needs and rights, two initial and parallel initiatives were decided. The first was strategic but with important practical potential; the second was practical with significant strategic opportunity. This first initiative was the complex and progressive business of finding community and enabling its emergence organizationally. There was much talk about community during the course of our workshops, about the search for identity and place, about making a community centre. It was a touchy issue that had animated everyone – more so than other priorities because it would challenge the authority and threaten the livelihood of the power elite (the water vendor, money lenders, informal utility suppliers and property owners) because no-one could decide if a centre were needed, what it would be, where it would go or who would run it.

Second, we were to build on the success of Mela's and Seva's work with solid waste management and recycling. It offered potential for enterprise and for environmental clean up. It gave opportunity to try out new forms of organization based on mutualization. It was a starter programme – an emergent organization waiting to be wired.

6

IN SEARCH OF COMMUNITY AND
THE STRUCTURE OF PLACE

*Places that happen, and happen to work; places that are made and don't
work; and the uncommonness of community.*

In cafes, at wells, in school playgrounds and at market places we
asked people to tell us about community – what is it, why we need
it and what it should be like. It was a first attempt to connect our
own theoretical understanding of community with experience
on the ground, which would help us understand and care for
community as an ideal, nurture it as a place and engage it as an
organization. We searched for those systems and networks, often
hidden, which give community its form and character, which we
might then use and build on to discipline our interventions. First
responses were all about place: a place for trading and networking,
some said, a waiting place – somewhere you know you've arrived.
A place for wasting time and for spontaneous events or chance
encounters or encounters by choice where public and private life
are mostly indistinguishable. It should be a place where the old can
sit and dream and pass on their wisdom and tell stories and gossip.
Somewhere not intimidating for women and children, where people
feel safe in the company of others because the surroundings are
familiar, because you don't get lost, because help is always at hand

and because you feel a sense of belonging. One man told of their village in the north, which had been raided by soldiers, resulting in his flight with his family across country to anonymity and the safety of the city. Their arrival at his brother's place was a triumph after the suffering of years of uncertainty and their untimely departure from home. They longed for another place called home where they could recapture their past and dream other futures. There were many of his kind, he said, scattered around the city – an invisible community. They had lost their homes and friends but retained the ideal of community in their collective memories.

In all of these first responses, the place people talked of had both physical and imagined boundaries. These imagined places seemed to liberate the mind, they helped build a collective meaning because they could be what the imagination conspires them to be rather than what planners say they ought to be. This is the soft city of dreams, expectation and hidden networks, about which Raban talks. 'The city as we imagine it, the soft city of illusion, myth, aspiration, nightmare is as real, maybe more real, than the hard city one can locate in maps and statistics, in monographs on urban sociology and demography and architecture'. And yet we know '...the built environment constitutes one element in a complex urban experience that has long been a vital crucible for the forging of new cultural sensibilities. How a city [place] looks and how its spaces are organized form a material base upon which a range of possible sensations and social practices can be thought about, evaluated, achieved'.[25]

Wandering around the area, doing our transect walks according to well-tried PRA techniques, we talk to others waiting at standpipes for water who had self-organized around clearing rubbish, maintaining their dusty cricket pitch and pirating electricity. In each case, a sense of community and organization emerged around common interests or crises; some groups had been long-standing, some had transformed and become a new group – a more formal organization with civic responsibilities assigned to it by the local authority – and yet others had come and gone. At the local temple (an ordinary shed converted roughly for prayer and religious festivals) another and more common kind of community was evident around common beliefs, around culture and ethnicity. At the other end of our site was a Lions Club with its own membership of individuals doing occasional charity work. And throughout, hundreds of small organizations and self-generating networks that had built a sense of belonging around work and trade.

During the days of listening, looking and, sometimes, measuring that followed, we tracked other clues to the structure of place, people and organizations that later, might become partners in development. We observed from one house the bundles of wire connected to one of the four electricity meters to the settlement. The man who had made the connections was an electrician working for the municipality and was selling electricity to others for a small connection charge and a monthly fee. This fee was calculated to maintain his monthly profit margins and bore little relationship to actual individual consumption. The charge per unit of consumption to households was, of course, much higher than those in the better-off parts of town. Round the corner, there was a bundle of hosepipes disappearing into the labyrinth of alleyways – providing a similar arrangement for selling on water. One man buys the supply from the water authority and sells it on, priced by the bucket, at a profit. In another corner we noticed two fire extinguishers proudly displayed at the front of a house. We talked to their owner who tells of a membership of some 20 families all within a five-minute dash of his place who, as with any insurance company, pay a weekly charge, which he collects, door to door, for fire-fighting service should there be need for one. In this dense part of the settlement, fires were common, largely provoked by kerosene-fuelled cooking stoves used in cramped conditions in houses built from wood, cardboard and plastics. He had attended three fires this last week. The community of neighbours had once organized a water storage tank to which people could rush with buckets in the event of a fire but the tanks were mostly empty. In the absence of water elsewhere, families used the supply not for fire fighting but for cooking, washing and the rest. And why did the city's fire brigade not attend the fires? The place was illegal, they were always busy enough elsewhere and, in any case, they couldn't get their vehicles in if they did arrive.

On a notice board outside one house, there was a list of names – a savings union. It was publicly on display to name and shame those who had defaulted on their instalments; more a protection racket, it first seemed, than a savings group. But, as it turned out, it was a group mostly of women – some 30 had joined – who were saving and borrowing in what they called a 'merry-go-round' way. Each week they would pay their instalment and every 30th week one of their members would get the jackpot for whatever purpose they desired.

In all these and other cases, there is a plethora of invisible stakeholders – the kind not attracted to workshops – and a diverse structure of community groups serving individual purposes by organizing collectively. In all these first observations and responses, the idea of community had both visible and invisible boundaries. Where to start? We take the easy option: something quick and visible, a catalyst to get everyone involved and show commitment. We were there to deliver!

We imagine a small building set in public open space – a place which gives collective status to the site, which can be recognized and named and properly managed, and be used by a new federation of community-based organizations which we were to help build. But who will own and manage it and how will this be decided? Where will it sit and what kind of facilities will it contain? We searched for precedents. One man gave us the example of his sister's place, some miles away, of a centre built with the help of a well-intentioned NGO which housed usefully a clinic, a childcare centre, a place for training young apprentices in needlework, for meetings and workshops.

Later that day we visited the centre. It was a simple structure built by local people using mud bricks for walls and clay tiles for roofs. Windows and doors had been scavenged from other building sites. The walls were rendered and decoratively painted in light blue, the window surrounds in a darker shade of blue. We were greeted by the centre's manager who showed us around. The building was impressive, a perfectly reasonable response to the needs of local inhabitants, so it seemed. The inside was clean and well ordered. In one room there was a row of young girls sitting at old Singer sewing machines making garments – part of a small enterprise set up by the NGO to create employment and generate funds for the centre's management and maintenance. It was a place where local women from rival ethnic groups met to sew and sell their tablecloths, tray cloths and napkins, etc. Another room housed the childcare centre, sparsely furnished with makeshift chairs and tables, its walls decked with children's drawings and paintings and its chairs with letters of the alphabet – in English. In the third room was the clinic. All perfectly reasonable.

But, beneath it all, there had been problems. For one thing, the new building had enhanced the status and power of a minority elite through the appointment of one of them to manage the centre. Blue was their ethnic colour and served to emphasize their authority, which was intimidating to others. It had all served to undermine existing and fragile leadership structures – of elders, religious leaders, landowners and entrepreneurs whose tacit rules of conduct had, over the years, enabled them all to differ but get along. It had cut deep divisions along class and ethnic lines. But they were well organized, and easy to find. For the NGO, it was an expedient partner, a practical choice, a community organization they could point to and work with. During the early stages of planning, our informant recalled, the team from outside used words to describe their intent which made a pleasant enough noise but did not mean much to the locals. They talked of empowering the poor, of partnerships between local stakeholders, of 'mobilizing an integrated leadership initiative' to manage the centre which would link community groups with the public authority – a public and private partnership encouraged by sponsors in search of good governance and sustainable development. They called it all a 'dynamically structured organizational model' offering both equity and efficiency in managing community affairs. None of these words translated well into the local vernacular and much had to be made up and was, no doubt, lost in translation. None of the ideas embodied in these phrases was easy to understand or assimilate.

When it was our turn to talk, he said, we explained to them our existing networks of informal organizations – of family members with mutual obligations to pool income, of friendship patterns and personal alliances, of home-based workers and collectives – they would become uncomfortable, even defensive. None of it fitted well with their concept of work or fairness. It all got too complicated. 'Things' were much easier to deal with and control than 'systems'.

Women, they said, were being subordinated and children exploited. Others – minorities and the poorest – were socially excluded. What we had were legitimized systems and powers which were the root cause of our poverty and ineptitude, which were the very systems and social structures they sought to disturb in favour of those more balanced in terms of gender, age, class, ethnicity – more democratic according to them. Other words like empowerment, enablement, participation or civic society were helpful to them, maybe, but not to us. All invoked ideals which served to help outsiders reinvent themselves and their organizations as development conquistadors, integrating new ideas into the jargon and abstraction which is the trademark of sustainable development – the equivalent of corporate branding – a sign of good quality and worthiness. Anyone can build houses, roads, put in water pipes and the rest. These things are today delegated to self-helpers, NGOs and local contractors, leaving the agencies with their academics and other consultants to focus on big ideas, to create a corporate mythology which reimagines development as environmental and political salvation, as social reawakening, all fuelled by careers and money and global politics.

In the end we got a building, a centre, he said. We went along with their ideas, nodded our way through endless meetings, talk shops and flip-chart presentations because, as always, getting something, we thought, is better than nothing and, besides, they had good intentions. It would have been impolite to question their wisdom and judgement, to challenge their authority. They were, after all, well educated. They had come a long way and were here to help.

And then there was the childcare centre and the sewing enterprise. Both had served to undermine existing home-based enterprises – a network of providers – of households everywhere working in dwellings, courtyards and streets. They had been denied the right to supplement their household income, the security or even survival of women was undermined in favour of an organization, an entity more easily accountable and manageable according to normative standards and internationally understood models of employment and enterprise. 'If women are engaged in making garments', said Ghafur in his research on home-based income generation, 'they do not supply them to city shops or agencies, which are essentially male domains; they prefer to sell the items themselves, house to house, and their clients are women'.[26] Our centre, managed by men, ignored the gender-specific focus of home-based work and serves to undermine women.

Throughout the settlement, and in informal settlements citywide, mothers had established a network of friends and other carers with whom they left their children. Each would pay a small fee to a needy and mostly elderly person who would take care of three or four children at once, for three or four hours a day. This network of home-based carers served to link parts of the settlement otherwise differentiated and sometimes divided by class, income or ethnicity. Carers were an important source of information to visiting mothers on where you could get cleaners, who could make furniture, mend or launder clothes or make garments. These were all additional sources of income generated by the movement of people across the usual economic and social divides which the centre and its centralized childcare service had disturbed.

* * *

Whilst figures vary from place to place, some 50 per cent of all poor households practise home-based income-generating activities of one kind or another. Whilst a household's total source of pooled income might be made up of waged labour, subsistence work, sale of commodities, rents and payment transfers (pensions, foreign receipts), some 50 per cent of household income is generated from home-based work. Much of this is generated by women. In India, for example, 94 per cent of women in poor areas might be self-employed in this way.[27] In Bangladesh, up to 60 per cent of household income is generated directly by women on their own or in collaboration with female members of their household, whereas 7 per cent is generated solely by men.[28]

'The goal [then] should be not to eliminate [or undermine] the practice of home-working, as it is clear that in many situations it is the only means by which women can make money, but to back up women organizing with policy that will increase their security', and in so doing, safeguard their community.[29] Access to credit and markets, basic education, training and the wider improvement of physical infrastructure – particularly transportation, water and electricity (all of which have been shown to have the greatest impact on household work) – confirm the need for broadly based approaches which generate money, build community and empower women. According to Ghafur: 'Credit given to a group of socially organized and well-motivated women, who will work and live in a physically improved environment with better health care is the bottom line of the contribution (which NGOs and public authorities can make) to household income generation.'[30]

And yet, despite years of progress in urban policy and management, of enabling frameworks, good governance and civil society in cities worldwide, street traders are rounded up and placed in compounds or cooperatives as a part of the city's clean up programmes (the *ambulante* in Lima or Guayaquil, for example). Settlers are displaced from their place of work, from their communities of practice and dumped on sites outside city centres (such as Bangkok, Cairo or Colombo), others are evicted and made homeless because they occupy sites designated for new roads or firebreaks, easements for dredging canals, or cemeteries, railway cuttings or rooftops. In Asia alone in 1996–1997, some 254,172 households (1.5 million people) were evicted and, for every household we can count, there will be at least two that go unreported. And so some 4.5 million people will have been displaced, one way or another, with some 25 million under threat of displacement.[31] Still today 'professional planners of highways, of redevelopment housing, of inner-city renewal projects, have treated challenges from displaced communities or community groups as a threat to the value of their plans, rather than as a natural part of the effort at social reconstruction'.[32]

* * *

And what of the clinic, I asked. How was that working? It was working well, we were told. There was another clinic a short ride away but getting there was difficult. 'And once there, we would often wait for hours to be attended. The trouble is, there is no bus service, we often lose a day's pay – those of us (most of us) on day rates – because of the time it all takes'. In their wisdom, the NGO had discovered that most problems are diarrhoeic and easily diagnosable and treated locally. They had trained a number of local women and men as paramedics who could easily diagnose and offer treatment. Where there was uncertainty, people would be referred back to the large and more fully staffed facility up the road. At first, separate days were allocated to each of the three social groups living here, each day staffed by their own respective and newly trained medics. Over time, these divisions had disappeared. The centre had organized health training sessions for women (and some men) in pre-natal care and around issues of better household water management and sanitation. These sessions were run by people carefully selected from all three social groupings and therefore served a community-development function as well. It served as a catalyst: a community of interest energizing around a common need. And later, as medics began home visits as well, they would be welcomed across entrenched social boundaries. Where once they were barriers – a place to hide, in the face of the threat from others, from evictions, the low self-esteem imposed by poverty or the real threat of class conflict – these new boundaries offered a sense of belonging and connectedness. They offered a common context of meaning where 'individuals acquire identities as members of a larger social network [where] the network generates its own boundaries'.[33] It was not yet extensive, nor widespread, but it was a start at social integration – 'a real way of surviving in an environment whose rationale has, like a dead language, become so obscure that only a handful of specialists (urban economists, sociologists, planners) can remember or understand'.[34] This, then, is the 'soft city' of dreams, expectations, interests held in common and webs of relationships, not easy to explain or model because its structure is largely invisible and, in any case, always changing.

'At first we, the community, were resentful of the small fee charged for visits to the clinic and thought them to be a part of the same process demanded by the IMF in their latest round of lending and structural adjustment programme – of charging fees for schools and hospitals which had halved the number of those attending schools and hospital visits. The clinic up the road, after all, was free and better staffed and equipped. But we came to understand', said the informant, 'that the money charged went to our own – the paramedics, trainers and community health workers – and to the management and maintenance of our own facility. This we were prepared to do. We have begun to build a community fund', he told us, 'offering much needed welfare support for the elderly'. Odd, though, we thought: a choice between convenience and service – a trade-off imposed on poverty which, in the end, we were bound to accept.

* * *

In the weeks and months that followed, I recalled the snapshots of literature one reads in those in-between times in search of theory and explanation. Social scientists have forever searched for some global definition which can caption the spirit and nature of community. In 1955, Hillary identified some 94 definitions.[35] In 1956, Koenig attempted a composite definition from all of these, suggesting 'a community is above all a global society of a kind that has a local unity, with an indefinite number of institutions, social groups and other phenomenon within it...'.[36] Interesting, I thought, but not yet very useful. Others think of community as 'a unit of society in place... where collectivity shares common experience, where the interests of people are localized... It is a place not only of economic activity and human association but it is also a place where memories are centred, both individual and folk memories'[37] – which gets us a bit closer, but not much.

Whatever the definition, five kinds of community emerge from the literature, which I find useful in practice and for which social scientists have names. All are interlinked – indeed we are all probably members of each.

The first is called 'community of interest'. In this context, people gather around issues of common concern or common advantage which they may agree as a basis for cooperation. Neighbourhood organizations get together to fight local developers or fight eviction, others to close streets to traffic, to collect rubbish or lobby the local authority for services and utilities. Some may exist without any formal structure, such as childcare groups, neighbourhood watches for fire, flood or crime, others are more formal with elected leaders, secretaries and treasurers. Some are activist, even political in motivation, and yet others are oppressive, centred on the trafficking of drugs or even people. These organizations may well seek a place to meet, they usually do: a community centre, a church hall, a local school, a dark basement or a hilltop. Others will invent a means of communication using ITC, newsletters or just street talk.

The second kind of community centres around culture – that 'integrated system of socially acquired values, beliefs and rules of conduct that delimit the range of accepted behaviour in any given society'. 'Communities of culture' are relatively homogenous and often structured according to social networks with shared values and beliefs which bind the network together:

> *The social network also produces a shared body of knowledge – including information, ideas and skills – that shape the culture's distinctive way of life in addition to its values and beliefs. Moreover, the culture's values and beliefs affect its body of knowledge. They are part of the lens through which we see the world. They help us interpret our experiences and decide what kind of knowledge is meaningful. This meaningful knowledge, continually modified by the network of communications, is passed on from generation to generation together with the culture's values, beliefs and rules of conduct.*[38]

The extent to which we are able to intervene and disturb communities of culture, in the interest of reshaping power relations according to today's development norms, remains contentious. But disturb them we do in our search for equity in gender relations, in democratizing government, in our emphasis on participatory planning and our notion of what makes good governance.

The third kind of community clusters around work. Capra calls these 'communities of practice'. As people pursue any shared enterprise over time, they develop a common practice: that is, shared ways of doing things relating to one another that allow them to achieve their joint purpose. Over time, the resulting practice becomes a recognizable bond among those involved. A social network emerges based on a shared purpose – 'a boundary of meaning and hence an identity... based on a sense of belonging' which, says Capra, is the defining characteristic of community.[39] Organizationally, cities are made up of clusters of communities of practice, some formal, most not. Their networks of informal enterprises, service providers and organizations are self-generating, self-organizing and flexible. 'The more people are engaged in these informal networks', says Capra, 'the more developed and sophisticated the networks are, the better will the organization be able to learn, respond creatively to unexpected new circumstances, change and evolve'. The sense of a city being alive resides in its communities of practice, as does its intelligence.

The fourth kind of community is held more in the mind and is not easy to find in place. West calls these 'communities of resistance'. They are 'created in the face of external threat, at times of social unease and change or under oppressive and hierarchical dominance'. Communities of resistance are 'where one is able to redeem and reclaim the past, legacies of pain, suffering and triumph in ways that transform present reality'.[40]

'I think that communities of resistance should be places where people can return to themselves more easily, where conditions are such that they can heal themselves more easily and recover their wholeness.'[41] City life, of course, is full of such communities who have either fled social and political conflict, who have been displaced by natural disaster or by a development project or, indeed, who face the daily threat of violence.

The fifth kind of community is place based. I do not propose here to dig deep into the abundant literature and theory about place-based communities. Four themes are, however, worth noting, especially given the early responses of people during our enquiry into their meaning of community.

First, and in cities, is the diminishing importance often allocated to place, where *awareness* of community takes precedent over *location*. Whilst all forms of community do have a spatial setting, in cities the idea is more networked rather than concentrated. In this sense, place is porous rather than confined.

Second, when it is geographically located, place often assumes more importance than space, especially for the poor and vulnerable. Security and accessibility take precedence over use value or identity, at least to start with.

Third, there is the relationship between place and identity. We see everywhere the appropriation of place in ways that empower community. Through territorial demarcation and use value, communities are also able to attach social value, coded with colour, boundary iconography and ornamentation. Our streets and squares everywhere give evidence to the status of place and the identity of community.

Finally, we should recognize the dynamic of time in our thinking and planning of place. In cities everywhere, we find communities of spontaneous place and also communities of temporal place. In the first case are the land invaders and squatter settlements which, over time, assume a sense of permanence. In the second are the mobile communities of pavement dwellers and street traders. Communities of temporal place, on the other hand, inhabit space for short periods of time – the playground or sports centre, the street market, the shoe cleaners or pavement barbers or the water point.

Whatever the type, community is mostly an ideal in development that we evangelize, something good and worthy, which distinguishes good guys from bad. It is a 'fine example of a motherhood word that produces a warm glow in listeners and elevates the speaker to a moral high ground'.[42] It is integral to the ritual of development, indeed a part of its mythology.

But community can be as much a part of the problem as a panacea. We have come to recognize, in recent research, that it 'hides many divisions and differences... [where] hundreds of millions are marginalized, oppressed and made miserable by discrimination and exclusion'.[43] In her paper, 'The rhetoric of the community in project management', Mfaniseni Sihlongonyane argues that communities are often oppressive to outsiders, a threat to minorities, to the individual, the unique, irregular, absent or incapacitated. She quotes John Beresford, who said: 'After 12 years of professional work I felt the need to get honest; my community-based organization didn't have a community, in any meaningful sense, and neither did most of the many other established associations I was in contact with at that time. It seemed that anything could be called 'community' but that no-one could point to their community'.[44]

During a study visit to Phnom Penh, one of my student groups working with rooftop squatters came to a similar conclusion:

> *Our group fell over ourselves trying to reconcile the different voices we heard during our interviews. I spent much of my time speaking with the Vietnamese residents who spoke at length about the discrimination they felt and their exclusions from the programmes offered to the Khmer*

majority population. Their needs for community seemed to centre on establishing parity with the Khmer in terms of numbers of public toilets or access to English language classes.

Meanwhile, other colleagues discovered that many of the Khmer residents they interviewed wanted to move from the rooftop. For some, this possibility was limited as their financial capital was tied up in a failing savings scheme; their priority was obtaining restitution, and then moving out. Nowhere did we hear that establishing better relationships with other residents was a priority, nor did we ever ask the question. Yet we persisted in pursuing an agenda that cited as an objective the creation of new communal spaces from which an increased sense of group cohesiveness would emerge. In effect it was the Cambodia variation of the Iowa Field of Dreams myth: if you build it, they will come.[45]

We are learning, however, to be cautious. Sarah Morgan, in her MPhil work on community, said:

I would argue that we need to be suspicious of community and the myriad of ambiguities that now surround it. We need to question whether notions of community have the right to develop as they do and debate the legitimacy of enabling community to gain broader rights over the individual and household in our current situation. We need to recognize that reification or re-romanticism of community is by no means a solution to social upheaval. No proximity of cultures is going to automatically build community, nor will advocating the right numbers and right sizes necessarily constitute the ideal community. Perhaps today the quest for community has to do with the need to modify strategies of change, to cultivate new coalitions in an attempt to bring about unity over the forms and functions of the city... Community is often represented as an entity in itself and neglected as being a part of a much broader social process that is occurring in our cities.[46]

This search for entity is a leftover from the old days of master planning. It ignores the continuance of shifting values and interest which are intergenerational and intercultural, of some whose notion of community is not just social and organizational but spiritual as well. And when it gets difficult to pin down, as it always does, we – the development practitioners – turn it all into something we do understand and can work with: an organization, a centre, a neighbourhood unit, a formal collective that can be a partner in that triad relationship between the state, the market and civil society. We attach to it a cognitive wholeness and then give it a hierarchal arrangement of leaders and managers with delegated roles and responsibilities and shared ideals which guide its purpose, an organization which is accountable, transparent and, according to some normative international standard, democratic. We bureaucratize it in ways that are understandable according to Northern logic and to all those serial thinkers who populate bureaucracy. We turn it into a thing that can be controlled. We give it responsibility but not too much authority. And then we invite it to participate in our decision-making process.

And why not?! 'Much of the world around us can be explained in terms of command systems and hierarchies... governed for the most part by pacemakers whether they are political leaders, council representatives, university vice-chancellors, company directors and the rest'.[47] But now we know that this kind of homogenizing of community with command systems gives a false sense of social and political identity to collectives and can be an agent of stereotyping designed to legitimize state or sectoral interventions. The treatment of local areas as communities of homogenous interests, said Lisa Peattie, way back in 1968 'can result in severe damage to the interests of the weakest inhabitants'.[48] There is an emerging consensus that we bypass the notion of community altogether in favour of a more direct link between household and civil society.

7

THE BUS STOP: CULTIVATING COMMUNITY

How starts can be stops, but also the other way round, as it turns out.

As we set about our planning we are, by now, cautious of pre-emptive community building. Instead, we seek to build an architecture of possibilities in the broadest sense of the term and give this shape, spatially and organizationally. Later, we may attach to it rules or codes of conduct which we will develop with others. In this way, we create the kind of social space where individuals and organizations engage with each other in ways more akin to the behaviour of Nakagakit's slime mould organism than any devised systems of planning. We create conditions, in other words, for emergence to take place and, in this respect, search for catalysts. The question for planners is: how much structure do we design before the structure itself interrupts the natural process of emergence?

We decide, as a first step, to explore the emergence potentials of the bus stop – to route the bus line, which currently skirts the area, into the site and provide a stopping place where the two roads on site intersect. Better transportation to city markets had been a priority need, in particular for those engaged in the fisheries business. It would be something quick, useful and visible. Better still, it would not require a loan from the World Bank to get it started. Located close by the chosen site is one of the settlement's few public standpipes where women and children gather to collect water, gossip and wash clothes. We might plant some trees to give shade where people wait or play and place some streetlights to give it all definition and make it look good.

We had observed elsewhere the density of life and commerce which clusters around places where buses stop. People will gather and wait for substantial periods of time and so, often and in small steps, small shops and coffee houses will open to serve them, shoeshine boys and other street hawkers will appear. These same people will carry their fish or other produce to city markets and will spread their baskets on the ground to sell what they can to passers-by while they wait. At first, a small market emerges: cheaply, spontaneously, incrementally and in response to demand and to circumstances. No-one designed a market place, no-one contrived a centre. Instead, conditions for trade were informally structured so that if it wanted to happen it could and, if not, very little investment was wasted and no-one would suffer. At the same time, with the newly installed streetlights, children would gather at night to do their homework, in the absence of lighting in their own homes. And where children gather, so do informal vendors selling candy, soft drinks, pencils and paper, exercise books and the rest. At the existing standpipe, more work and organization to integrate this facility into this new place are done – a new water trust had been set up and improvements to this, and other water supply facilities, were under way. Later, we would seek to find a place for Mela's new waste management resource centre and expand this to include a meeting place for all the organizations now working in this settlement.

At a chance encounter with the Dean of the National University's Faculty of Medicine and Dental Surgery, we persuaded the school's dental department to offer their services to the community as part of their field training. We would provide a place for their mobile dental unit to park once a week, adjacent to the new resource centre, which was also now used for community events and meetings. It was a visible event that attracted many – to look if not to be treated – with free inspection and advice.

In time, the word got around that there was cheap and fresh food to be had at this daily informal market. As its reputation as a fish market grew, so people would come from town to buy. Buses were now bringing people in and not just taking people out. It became known as The Fish Run. Meanwhile, the firemen's cooperative, a long-standing organization set up to look after the welfare of its members, would get together with the newly set up water trust and Mela's waste management organization to elect a new Council of Community Representatives to help develop the commercial potential of their centre – to pool a community enterprise revolving fund in partnership with the local authority to secure their new school, improve utilities, encourage fire prevention and put in place flood-prevention measures. It was all based on the initiatives of Seva, who had for some time been running a day bank for small businesses, mainly pavement hawkers.[49] The bank encourages individuals and small groups to save small amounts of money and, in contrast to the high interest rates charged by money lenders (10–20 per cent) enables small loans at interest rates of around 0.5 per cent. Loans had ranged from between R1000 to R20,000 and the operation was simple: each day, members borrow what they need to buy stock or materials and pay it back at the end of the day. The new Council of Community Representatives would be encouraged to establish a day bank to support household programmes in recycling and other enterprises related to the community's new and emergent Centre.

One such entrepreneur was Tandia's son, Tomi, whose rudimentary skills at carpentry, together with a loan of R3000, enabled him to convert his bicycle into a delivery vehicle. He had tied a wooden box to the back and insulated this with polystyrene sheets, which he had bought from Mela's recycling centre. He had decorated the box with small advertisements for which he got a few pennies. With its growing reputation as a fish market, he would set out at 5.00am to go to the bus stop, buy his fresh fish from the still informal market, take it home, scale, clean and sometimes fillet the fish before packing it in ice into his box. By 7.00am he was on the road delivering orders or touting for sales, mostly in the middle-class parts of town. At the end of each day, he would pay back his loan and earn a profit of between R500 and R800, which he invested back into his business. In time, he and his friends would own a fleet of 12 bicycles and offer deliveries of vegetables and dairy products, picked up from households and, over time, create network markets for families producing a few eggs, a dozen tomatoes or a bundle of carrots. Tomi and his fleet of individual entrepreneurs, who collectively had enhanced their commercial potential like any other growing business, parked their bicycles close to where the buses stop – which became known, like a taxi rank, as a place where you could always find delivery bikes. Unsurprisingly, as the delivery bikes would return to home base, so the business of maintenance and repair would emerge. Nearby and soon enough, front rooms and courtyards were converted into repair shops; others for calligraphy, making small signs, and even making sun hoods for bikes. It became more openly a place to get your bike fixed, a place to buy a new bike made out of recycled parts, some from Mela's centre, a place to hire bikes to carry people and food when you could not, at first, afford your own. Soon, Tomi found himself returning from his daily run selling fish with school uniforms for mending, with a special order for leather bible covers, and with information on who needs cleaners in the smarter parts of town, or childcarers or cooks or gardeners. His networking of markets and people, his entrepreneurship, his source of information had, in many ways, enabled him to become a development practitioner in his own right. His organization was emerging and scaling up.

8

PICKERS, SORTERS AND TAP ATTENDANTS

In which Mela turns other people's rejects into one great big enterprise and becomes herself a social entrepreneur.

Located close to where the buses stop, on derelict land, was another source of energy and opportunity clustered around an existing but intermittent standpipe, one of the few in this part of town. There were various clues which got us thinking. For one thing, it was curious to see a line of colourful buckets arranged in orderly fashion but with none of their owners in attendance. A couple of young girls were darting about playfully, keeping a watchful eye on the buckets, and curious themselves that we should be curious. What was striking was not so much the absence of water (a common occurrence, an acceptable hardship in the context of all else), but rather that people would trust to leave their buckets unattended without fear of losing their place in the line-up or, indeed, losing the buckets. There was, it seemed, some semblance of organization implied in the order of buckets, some purpose to our playful young girls. It mitigated, it seemed, the risk of theft, something to build on perhaps, as we considered extending the network to other parts of the settlement and having it properly managed.

For another thing, and to one side, laundry hung on a makeshift line of insulated electric wire, composed mostly of large bed sheets and linen pillow-cases, grey with years of washing in muddy water – items of laundry one would not normally associate with domestic life, not here at least. Large galvanized steel buckets, some five or six, lay nearby, giving hint to some form of enterprise. A small and hopelessly inadequate 2-metre-square cemented apron had been built as a surround to the standpipe, to drain away spillage, but that was cracked and in disrepair. All around, there were puddles on the ground, evidence that there would be water again.

We talked to the two girls who told us that they earned a little pocket money by keeping an eye on things. The issue was less one of security than, when water did come (and no-one knew exactly when this would be), the buckets needed to be filled so that they could be collected later by their owners. The bed linen, they said, belonged to a couple of local guesthouses. A small collective of women had set themselves up to provide laundry services. There had been some considerable argument about the amount of time the women occupied at the tap and the amount of water they consumed, which often denied others. Their earnings contributed nothing to the operation and maintenance of the standpipe – a public facility for private gain without advantage to others. Local families and the laundry collective shared one common concern, however. Both groups were resentful of the local authority that had failed to maintain the supply, let alone extend this to other parts of the settlement. The girls, we recognized, were operating as tap attendants, an individual and ad-hoc arrangement with potential, it seemed, for social enterprise, particularly in our planning for the extension of the network.

I recalled the example of Water Aid's project in Hitosa, Ethiopia, as a starter in our planning.[50] In Hitosa, water committees were set up and tap attendants appointed to look after the taps and manage water sales. The whole was run by women who were trained in basic skills of management and accountancy. Tap attendants lived close to their respective taps and at first took 60 per cent of the proceeds of water sales as income. Later, they settled for a wage equivalent to the national minimum, which guaranteed a regular payment. Tap attendants sold water at 5 cents for every 40 litres through a system of vouchers. Local water committees were set up which, in conjunction with a water management board and a water administration office all made up of local people, managed the network. Meters were installed on each tap to monitor consumption and to check on monies deposited after sales and after allowing for some 4 per cent in wastage of water. The water management board, made up of trained women from the community, oversaw this social enterprise and, in addition, extended their services into health education.

At another action planning workshop, we brought together the municipal authority responsible for water, and some of the other vested interest groups, including those already selling water via illegal hosepipe connections. Nina, Tandia, Mela and the Council of Community Representatives were all present. We looked to adopt and adapt the lessons from Hitosa and facilitate the emergence of a water management organization closely related to the physical and spatial organization of the water network itself. We sought to generate a layout for the settlement based on distinguishable, yet easily inter-related levels of organization – facilitating partnerships in the design, implementation, management and maintenance of the network.

The settlement would be divided into five clusters, each managed by a cluster committee of elected volunteers – the equivalent of the local water committee. Each cluster would have four standpipes, each managed by a tap attendant. A representative from each cluster would sit on a water management board (five members) which would become a sub-committee to the Council of Community Representatives. The network itself would include the laying of mains water pipes 6 inches in diameter along lines of major access, with 3-inch and 2-inch diameter pipes branching to each of the standpipes. Individual connections to households would be facilitated by the cluster committee, if needed. The municipality would be responsible for the 6-inch main, the water management board for installing and maintaining the branch network. At the same time, four additional standpipes were located along the commercial lines of major access, managed and maintained by the board in partnership with the municipality. Two of these were located at the intersection where the buses stopped and would be designated, substantially, for commercial enterprise. A small shelter was erected and paid for by the local authority. Meters would be attached to all standpipes to monitor consumption.

Adjacent to the water shelter, Mela's recycling enterprise – in partnership with the local school, the local authority and the water management board – opened a water resource centre selling recycled water-related products: buckets for carrying water, home-based storage tanks in case of flood or shortage, water bottles for collecting rainwater and odd bits of hosepipe. Exhibited also was the latest from Mela's recycling resource centre – an improvised hot-water tank from recycled parts, fuelled by charcoal. On a notice board there were announcements of training sessions on how to make your own.

Encouraged by the municipality and with the help of our NGO partner, the water management board had embarked on health training and awareness programmes, involving children in teaching and spreading health and hygiene-related activities. Ten core trainers of women were trained and employed by the municipality at the water resource centre who, in turn, started their training of children at the same school where, later, Tandia would begin her nutrition programme. In time, a number of primary schools joined the network, and set up child-to-child training clubs which enabled children to discuss and formulate health strategies with teachers who would guide and facilitate. The schools' health outreach pro-grammes would occasionally locate at the water resource centre, for events and displays that the children would organize for the wider community.[51] For the logo, they adapted the adage 'Children should be seen AND heard'. Water, sanitation and health would become integral parts of the 'education for development' programme.

What started as a practical need to supply water, ended with the inclusion of a wider, more strategic agenda of enterprise, skills development, health education and community organizing, involving children, community organizations, the municipality and local schools.

With the establishment of markets, bus stops, recycling enterprises, cafes, bike shops, a water enterprise and other things, property values slowly began to increase around the Centre. Some who had been poor took advantage by renting front rooms to shopkeepers, to tailors, bakers or set up more coffee shops. Others cashed in and moved elsewhere, preferring to invest their gains in schooling for children or setting up a new business.

Meanwhile, since her return from Bangkok, Mela had been working hard to set up her recycling enterprise. There had been some considerable scepticism about the real potential of waste as income, despite examples which she had documented from her study trip. But she did manage to mobilize a small core of people to show how it could be done. With the help and goodwill of the deputy director of the municipality's public works department whom she had met during her trip, and with the facilitation skills of Seva, she managed to collect, over a three-month period, enough paper, cardboard, glass and metals to make her first sale. Both Seva and the municipality helped open doors to two private companies that buy paper and glass. Mela and her group made their first sale, equivalent to around US$22 – small but it would become significant.

News of the sale spread to other parts of the area and, before long, others had joined in and were doing it. The volume of waste collected tripled in quantity over the next few months. It became clear that their own organizational arrangements would need to adapt to their new scale of enterprise. Something was needed which could become settlement-wide and, if it were to succeed, would need to be formally contracted: a community contract with the municipality with mutual obligations and responsibilities, whilst avoiding the usual pyramid structure that larger organizations tended to adopt. It needed to set prices for materials and set up systems of payment to households with proper and transparent accounting. It needed to establish a permanent collection centre for waste to be sorted and stored. It needed a marketing plan.

Mela's entrepreneurship and energy, and her track record, enabled her to negotiate a deal with the city's land reclamation and development corporation for a plot of land of around 250 square metres, which they were to lease to build a new recycling centre. Once negotiated, it was not difficult to persuade the Ministry of Urban Development and Housing, as well as the municipality's sustainable cities programme, to join in and to share the cost of a new building. They agreed, on condition that the new enterprise deposited some 20 per cent of the overall cost of the building – equivalent to around US$400 as a down payment. This they secured with a loan from Sevantha, which they would repay in part with their own skilled labour and in part with profits from the sale of waste. At the same time, the NGO organized a programme of training in book-keeping and, importantly, in the collection and sorting of waste. Paper, cardboard, glass and metals all had their own market value according to weight and quality, as did the variety of plastics dumped for waste.

As for the building itself, another chance encounter with the National University's School of Architecture engaged students to make proposals for a building, which would be a model of appropriate technology and energy efficiency. The task, to use substantially recycled materials and at the same time make it all look new – a piece of architecture, not just another building, something that could be exhibited at the city's town hall, which would attract visitors and give the place status.

Over the months that followed, groups of women were separately contracted as waste pickers, armed with gloves and overalls and hand-drawn carts for collecting material, supplied by the department of public works. At the Centre itself, a separate team of community workers were contracted to do the sorting according to market demand. Private companies were now placing orders for specific types of waste – a sale was negotiated every few months.

As time went on, other pickers joined the business and, at first, attempted to sell directly to private companies. They soon realized that the volume of waste needed to be collected to be profitable was far greater than they could collect individually and joined the Centre's enterprise with income starters (small loans to get businesses or small enterprises started) secured through the Council of Community Representatives' enterprise fund. A clear, transparent survey of prices for materials was regularly pinned to the notice board outside the new centre – their own local stock market!

Before long, new programmes emerged for generating enterprise around product development encouraged at the Centre, with new machinery bought to process material before sale and by a new link we established with the local University's Industrial Design department. The Centre served for a while as a laboratory for students working with, and training, local young people. Their apprenticeships would be certified by the University, helping them establish new enterprises and indeed gain employment with the larger and formal materials processors and manufacturers. For students, this was hands-on and invaluable experience toward their university qualification. As in Thailand, Mela's enterprise soon extended into schools, with contracts to collect waste and with regular workshops for children. They made books with coloured covers out of recycled paper and, at the same time, were taught the value of recycling – that stuff you throw away can be fun and profitable. These books, cards, gift boxes and mobiles, were sold at an occasional stall near the Centre, where the buses stopped, and earned enough money over time to make their own contribution for a new goal post and basketball hoop – a sports centre close to their school leased by the municipality, well protected and self-managed, as they had agreed. They had earned their sports centre and, with it, a place in the governance of a public facility.

* * *

Examples of the successes of these kinds of social enterprise and entrepreneurship, of moving from user to partner in a progressive process of mutualization, of scaling up quantitatively, functionally, politically and organizationally, can be found everywhere and not just in developing countries. In London in 1996, for example, Ealing Community Transport set up ECT Recycling which now offers a diverse range of recycling services including the first ever paint exchange scheme. From a small non-profit start, ECT has since diversified into a group comprising four separate companies, employing over 200 staff and providing recycling and community transport services for eight local authorities – six in London and two outside. It is the national pioneer in kerbside recycling and provides direct services to over 425,000 households. Its current group turnover of £13 million is increasing at over 20 per cent per year.[52] Whilst some of these enterprises begin through volunteerism or activism, they survive because they earn money, their members work as partners with public authorities, and the enterprise is owned and governed by its members. They are participatory, profitable and decentralized, and represent still a new deal, a new social contract for the provision of housing, services and utilities. In countries of the South, they are the mainstream, with enormous latent emergent potential.

9

THE PICKLE JARS

How Tandia's cucumbers grew and grew... and just kept on growing into schools and markets.

The Council of Community Representatives' newly established enterprise fund set about its task of generating work and money in the sustainable and mutual way its members had agreed: that is, with careful attention to social enterprise, economic development and the environment. Their initial task was to sort out what needed to be done and with whom, in ways that would enable small enterprises to emerge and grow. They wanted to know more about who was already doing what, how existing small businesses got started and what was stopping others from getting started. What skills were under-utilized, what natural resources were at hand? Later, they will want to know, in respect to it all, what equipment, working capital or start-up cash is needed? Who might benefit from working with whom? What is getting in the way of people starting up businesses, finding jobs, building houses, getting their children to school, obtaining proper health care and so on? Do local regulations impose restrictive taxes on employment? Do building permits still take months to approve? Are there still restrictions on land ownership, the use of common land, trading, renting, keeping animals? And how do people cope with the shocks and stresses of natural disasters, everyday hazards or social exclusion? What, in this sense, is the extent of their vulnerability? And, given the ethnic mix in the area, what are social and cultural practices regarding work in each of the different ethnic groups, how do they organize and what are their attitudes to cooperation?

And, all the time, the enterprise fund is searching for ways to join people and organizations together, build ties in some circumstances and loosen ties in others, expand the scale of small initiatives, open doors to ideas, to other people, to organizations who can help find money and expertise, reframe questions, legitimize and give status. And also to be rigorous, flexible and principled, working sometimes with individuals for the collective good and not always with communities. And, importantly, as one goes about one's work, learning that sometimes it may be best just to leave things alone.

As work got underway – led by community volunteers – we encountered one enterprise, easy to miss, the smallest I have seen, along one of the many hidden pathways leading to the Centre. Two glass jars (which I recognized as those used to sell boiled sweets in newspaper shops in England in the 1950s, a remnant of past days) sat on a child's stool in the sun. The stool was made of old boxwood, put together with rusty nails and an odd array of metal angles and straps. It was sturdy and well crafted. The jars contained five pickled cucumbers each, which were for sale to passers-by. The whole was easy to pass by as irrelevant to our task, too small to make a difference in the face of our bigger goal – to create a sustainable environment for social and economic development and wellbeing in this expanding but deprived urban settlement.

Tandia, who owned the jars, showed us into her small house built from material scavenged from anywhere and everywhere. She was a recent arrival and lived with her two sons, Tomi (who we met earlier) and Fen. At the back of her house was a tiny courtyard of about 18×18 metres in which stood three large flowerpots – the source of her produce. Continuity in producing, then pickling cucumbers was obviously difficult, given her limited capacity to grow the raw material. But she also grew some herbs that we saw drying in the back and there was a tomato plant as well. It was all a tiny venture, earning equivalent to some US$3–4 a month, which, combined with her cleaning work, her occasional work at making school uniforms (she was part of a recently convened cooperative that was now bidding for school contracts), Tomi's carpentry and bike repairs skills, and her younger son's hair-cutting business, brought the household income to around US$30 a month.

Stashed also in her backyard were some tools for fixing bicycles, and bits of wood, metal and bicycle parts, as well as her younger son's barber's chair and his hair-cutting equipment – a mirror, a comb, a pair of scissors and a shaving brush and razor for doing beards. The barber's chair had been put together by Tomi, built on four wheels taken from a child's old bicycle, so that it could be easily dragged from place to place in search of custom. The boy would go out every morning dragging his chair with him and would park it against a wall or fence – designated places which he had informally claimed with a sign on the wall announcing his opening times and which had become familiar to locals as places where you could get your hair cut. On his way out, he would pick up a free newspaper from the newspaper place he passed, free because it was from the day before, a throw-out. This he would offer his customers whilst they waited for haircuts, in the shade of an old bed sheet that he had attached to the wall. No one worried that the news was yesterday's or even the day before. In the overall continuum of things, a day or so behind on news, current affairs and gossip was generally of no consequence to people whose lives more generally were also and forever a day or so behind, or so it seemed – who would return tomorrow to find out what happened today. It was the kind of time warp his customers and he were used to, people whose lives and aspirations were full of yesterdays and tomorrows, so much easier to make sense of and live with than all the hardships of today.

There was an air of 'exotic chaos' about Tandia's house and yard, a hive of industry, resourceful and inventive. What they lacked was opportunity and connectedness, a community of practice that would make them money and give them status. Their industry was waiting to emerge.

In our discussions, Tandia talked of others like herself, mostly elderly people in her street, who grew a few vegetables to feed themselves and would occasionally sell surplus on their doorsteps. They had talked often of pooling their resources and sharing out responsibilities – you grow tomatoes, I'll do herbs and cucumbers, you cultivate cabbages or cauliflowers, and so on. They had already begun what outsiders called a cooperative of urban farmers and managed a stall at the local market – where the buses stopped – but it was difficult to keep it going. There wasn't the capacity or money to make a real go of it. Besides, they got into squabbles over how to divide up profits from sales, which were in any case no more substantial than when they were doing it all alone.

As she talked, my imagination began to wander. Some days earlier, we had visited the local primary school on our progressive rounds of looking and listening – the same school where Mela was doing her recycling workshops – and talked to the rather dispirited headteacher. Her planned art building had been indefinitely postponed because of the usual round of government spending cuts. 'Educating the Senses', it seemed, engaging the senses with the physical and natural world, was always expendable, an optional extra.

The demise of the school's art's centre had made available a piece of land that could, in the meantime we thought, be cultivated with plants and vegetables – an enterprise for the elderly maybe, linked to an awareness programme for children in plant cultivation and nutrition. Malnutrition was, after all, a problem identified during the planning workshop. It was the start to a new community-based programme, which could then lead to a citywide initiative in Education for Sustainable Development, linking environmental ecology to health, enterprise and social development. We were to recall, by way of examples, the work done by the Botanic Garden and Research Institute in Kerala, India, and in particular its Herbs For All and Health For All, and its Plants For All and Wealth For All programmes.[53] Food security, awareness programmes on diet, nutrition, hygiene, training on growing multiple plant species representing local plant diversity were all-important characteristics. There are now growing educational initiatives worldwide. In England, for example, the Oxfordshire Educational Authority has recently launched its own Learning to Last strategy for schools and, in New York, the Bronx Green-up project, which serves some 325 community gardening projects around the city, promotes a garden or greening project at every public school in the Bronx and 'works to establish a network of gardening teachers who can support and inspire each other'. I had visited similar school grounds in Zambia and South Africa. But here it would need larger-scale funding and political support – a network of international partners maybe. I reflected on our experience in Guayaquil in Ecuador and wondered if there were lessons and partners there, that we could use here.

In Ecuador it was a programme to regenerate the city of Guayaquil physically, socially and economically. Integrated into this programme were opportunities for tourism, environmental conservation and livelihoods on Santay, an island of about 180 people lying a few minutes off the mainland in the Guyas estuary. We had worked with the community and other partners – the navy, the municipality, an environmental NGO, an urban foundation of city fathers – to put a plan together. We needed to be inventive and entrepreneurial in winning political support and raising funds for the project. I recalled our discussion with Shell and its foundation in London, and their newly found corporate responsibility to environmental issues; Coca Cola and its foundation supporting education; the Global Environmental Facility in Washington, set up after the 1992 Rio Earth Summit on Environmental Sustainability, which might support feasibility work; and the British government through its debt conversion scheme, redirecting debt into projects promoting environmental sustainability, poverty reduction and education. Then there was the Eden Project in England, with its experience in managing facilities and promoting all kinds of programmes in environmental conservation, shelter and education.

It was all at once ambitious and imaginable. What if, we asked, these same organizations became partners in education for sustainable development, an alliance of local, national and global institutions in the governance of education? Who would win and who might lose out? What might happen to Tandia and her colleagues if big money and big organizations got involved? We decided to get it all going first in a small way, without outside help and later, maybe, involve others when we were ready to scale up.

With the technical help of botanists from our local university, another action planning workshop was organized, attended by community people brought together with the help of Tandia, teachers and NGOs, to develop an action plan for the vacant land and the school programme. It would be a demonstration project for others, citywide. The land (some 600 square metres) would be planted in two ways: at one end there would be a medicinal and ornamental plant garden, at the other (and comprising its major part) there would be vegetables. The garden would be supplied with compost from Mela's composting centre (which would expand its supplies to other schools as the programme expanded). The garden would be managed by a new Greening Enterprise, chaired initially by Tandia with her committee of elders and including representatives from the community, the students, teachers and the municipality. It was a partnership between the school, the public authority, the children and the community. It would be managed by the elderly as a part of their welfare programme. They would make a little money and regain their dignity. Tandia and her colleagues would look at ways of working with children, to prepare school meals from the local produce, as far as possible, and, as they did so, children would learn about the nutritional value of plants and pick up skills as well. It would all become a regular part of the weekly curriculum on sustainable education. Later, and in view of the success of this pilot, other schools citywide might take similar initiatives – a network of green enterprises would emerge and the Education for Sustainable Development programme would get underway nationally and consolidate globally.

Meanwhile, back on site, Tandia's sons chased their own dreams. Tomi, we know, had taken advantage of the fish market with his fish run and delivery fleet. He had rented a small space near to where his fleet of delivery bikes were parked, where he sold bicycle parts and accessories – all recycled – and where he ran one of the bike repair shops that had sprung up. His younger brother, Fen, had moved in with his hair-cutting business and set up shop in one corner. He now rented his mobile unit to a cousin who borrowed from the day bank to get started and who took over his hair-cutting patch as the business began to expand. Outside the shop, Tomi and his brother put up a colourful sign, which proudly read 'Barber's Shop. We Also Sell Bicycle Parts'.

* * *

During the course of the following years, encouraged by the government's new 'support based' policy for urban development – conceived, designed and implemented through years of trial and error, with the participation of local people and in partnership with all those others who can help technically, politically, financially – settlements countrywide adopted similar methods.

Last year, I sat in on a meeting of the city's planning and housing department, chaired by the mayor. All around were city officials and the chairpersons of the hundreds of community development councils citywide who had federated and gained legal status in the legislator of the municipality. They engaged in discussion on needs, raised issues and problems which their members faced, challenged public and private institutions on land development which disadvantaged their members, lobbied for resources for new schools or school programmes and for land rights. There were negotiations on new tariffs for utilities, on new tax laws on home-based enterprise and other informal businesses. A new form of governance had emerged with the support structure, which was designed to enable it all.

Not all small beginnings achieve strategic value. Indeed most times, strategic change is hard to come by – the filter upwards of ideas and learning clogs with those who will resist change and those with old-style laws and regulations left over from days of old-paradigm thinking. The connectedness it all demands between events and organizations doesn't happen because people are still dependent, or because they have only recently won their independence and are not yet ready to move to interdependence. But none of this diminishes the importance of the effort and the gains on the ground.

PART 3
LEARNING PRACTICE

'ALL PEOPLE ARE DEAD, SAVE FOR THOSE WHO KNOW; AND THOSE WHO know are dead, save for those who practise; and those who practise are all astray save for those who act with right intentions; and those who act with right intentions are all in grave danger.'

Dhu'l Nun, *A Treasure of Traditional Wisdom*[1]

10

PLAN–ANALYSE–SURVEY: PLANNING FROM BACK TO FRONT

In which the planner weighs street-level action against taking the long view, and comes down finally and firmly in the middle.

What lessons can we learn for elsewhere? What do these ordinary and everyday stories tell us about practice? What do they explain or confirm about process and about governance? Where is practice best placed, driven as it is by need and the imperative of rights, to connect practical work with strategic work, freedom with order, small-scale organizations with large-scale organizations, top-down coordination and bottom-up design?

In our case examples we have searched throughout for ethical associations and symbiotic relationships between organizations large and small, public and private; between the 'I' we call individual and the 'we' we call society. Architects, planners and social and political scientists have always recognized these tensions as endemic to practice. They called for a convergence of opposites and an association of differences for mutual benefit in the design of policy, spatial plans and buildings. What is recognized is the need for both opposites, not either/or. What we need is an understanding of 'natural scales and limits' in order that polarities can co-exist. 'Creativity and life are the result of tension between opposites', said Kaplan. 'Harmony is attained not through resolution but through an attunement of opposite tensions... slipping into one or other of two polarities... heralds the supreme danger of fundamentalism in which only one side of any polarity is recognized as having validity'.[2] In his book *Tools for Conviviality* Illich explored the relationship between technology and industrial production and how both could serve rather than dominate people:

> *When any enterprise grows beyond a certain point... it frustrates the end for which it was originally designed and then rapidly becomes a*

threat to society itself... We must come to admit that only within limits can machines take the place of slaves; beyond these limits they lead to a new kind of serfdom. Only within limits can education fit people into a manmade environment: beyond these limits lies the universal schoolhouse, hospital ward or prison... Once these limits are recognized, it becomes possible to articulate the triadic relationship between persons, tools and a new collectivity.[3]

Illich's concerns were reflected also by social and political scientists and by economists. Berger and Neuhaus, for example, wrote in 1977:

For the individual in modern society, life is an ongoing migration between two spheres, public and private. The mega structures are typically alienating, that is, they are not helpful in providing meaning and identity for individual existence... Whilst the two spheres interact in many ways, in private life, the individual is left very much to his own devices, and thus is uncertain and anxious... The dichotomy poses a double crisis. It is a crisis for the individual who must carry on a balancing act between the demands of the two spheres. It is a political crisis because the mega structures (notably the state) come to be devoid of personal meaning and are therefore viewed as unreal, or even malignant.[4]

These same issues led Schumacher, among others, to conclude:

In the affairs of men there always appears to be a need for at least two things simultaneously, which on the face of it seem to be incompatible and to exclude one another. We always need both freedom and order. We need the freedom of lots of small autonomous units, at the same time, the orderliness of large scale, possibly global unity and coordination... What I wish to emphasize is the duality of the human requirement when it comes to the question of size: there is no single answer. For his different purposes, man needs many different structures... for constructive work, the principle task is always the restoration of some kind of balance.[5]

Planners and architects reflected similar concerns. It was Ebenezer Howard, after all, who in 1898 sought to reconcile freedom and order in his garden cities and to 'dispense the minimum of organization that would secure the benefits of planning while leaving to individuals the greatest possible control over their own lives. He hated bureaucratic paternalism... [and] realized that planning must stay within self-imposed limits'.[6] The architect John Turner in his book *Housing by People* came to the same conclusions about scales and limits based on his ground-breaking work in Peru where he formulated his own principle on scales and limits which he called planning for housing through limits. 'Only if there are centrally guaranteed limits to private action can equitable access to resources be maintained and exploitation avoided. As long as planning is confused with design and lays down lines that people and organizations must follow, enterprise will be inhibited, resources will be lost, and only the rich will benefit'.[7]

In housing, it was the architect John Habraken who gave all this physical form and linked these themes to modes of housing design and production. He also recognized in his work the important reasoning between scales of organization and the need to reconcile opposites in the social and physical production of housing. He called his larger framework of things 'supports' which would represent shared values and which would be decided upon by collectives and public authorities. And he called all the bits that would turn this framework into homes 'detachable units'. He recognized that decisions about how much structure and infill there should be would largely depend on prevailing power relations and therefore on a good understanding of the prevailing political and social context – on what people were able or willing to do for themselves, which would always be different from place to place. All this he linked to modes of production. Supports would mobilize one system of producers and one scale of operations, and detachable units another. The task was to ensure both realms were technically and socially compatible.

More recently, we have turned our attention to the natural sciences for explanation, we have looked at chaos theory, emergence and the study of complexity.

Waldrop captioned nature's complex systems in his discussion on complexity. He called this 'The emerging science at the edge of order and chaos'.[8] On the one hand is the structure, cohesiveness and coherence of systems which give us order and stability, not easily explained by chaos theory; on the other is the spontaneity, adaptability and self-organizing which, like the human brain, enables species, institutions and industry to evolve and survive based on experience and learning, enabling them to be creative and novel in response to need.

In our examples from previous pages we have witnessed this creativity and novelty at various levels of organization in response to an environment disturbed by practice, and triggered by events or other intervention. For Capra, this process involves several stages:

> [T]o begin with, there must be a certain openness... a willingness to be disturbed in order to set the process in motion; and there has to be an active network of communication... to amplify the triggering event. The next stage is the point of instability, which may be experienced as tension, chaos or crisis. At this stage, the system may either break down or it may break through to a new state of order, which is characterized by novelty...[9]

The first stages of openness – the willingness to be disturbed – we explored in the early phase of action planning, in our search for problems and opportunities and in our assessment of urban risk. We must recognize also that much of the early work with PRA dominantly serves that purpose. But openness has to be nurtured, through trust building, which is a key phase in our action planning programme. The early exercises, in street work or workshops, enable us to assess the extent to which people are open to change and are willing to participate with each other, in search of change and in search of novelty. It enables outsiders to focus their efforts where need is greatest and together to search for triggers for change. Our bus stop, our pickle jar and our water lines are all examples – they are all triggers in their own right, once recognized.

The sheer inevitability of her plight of eviction moved Mela to a state of openness to resettlement. She became willing to be disturbed and therefore willing to engage resettlement, out of necessity at first, not by choice. At the same time, she became uncertain, maybe confused, a little fearful, because things, people and places were going to be different. An active network of communication and feedback was already in place in the form of the eviction hotline. As they connected with others to lobby and build, so new organizations emerged which needed some designing. In a different way, we see a similar process of emergence in new ways with the pickle jars, the barber's shop, the fish run and delivery fleet, the community water board and the recycling centre. In turn, as they became connected together themselves in loose and sometimes informal ways, so an even larger order of structure emerged in the form of the Council of Community Representatives – a new order of governance emerged citywide that had formal status at city council meetings.

It is a cyclical, progressive and non-linear process, emerging exponentially. In our planning and site work throughout, one recurring theme dominates: the relationship between structures we design and those which are enabled to emerge. This was the theme, in a different way, faced by Illich, Schumacher and others in their various comments on scales and limits, and more recently by Capra in his discussion on the relationship between emergence and design. 'Human organizations always contain both designed and emergent structures', he says:

> *The designed structures are the formal structures of the organization (city)… the emergent structures are created by the organizations' (city) informal networks and communities of practice… designed structures provide the rules and routines that are necessary for the effective functioning of the organization… Designed structures provide stability. Emergent structures, on the other hand, provide novelty, creativity and flexibility. They are adaptive, capable of changing and evolving… The issue is not one of discarding designed structures in favour of emergent ones. We need both.*[10]

This, then, was the challenge faced by Patama in her designs for resettlement and also in our planning of the water network. For Patama, the designed structure at first took on physical form. Later, it developed into guidelines, designed by the larger collective in response to their shared need to agree standards to safeguard light and privacy, which would avoid conflict. All of this facilitated the emergence of novelty in house design. In a similar way, the water network, designed to grow in time, enabled other and complementary emergent structures to form, triggered by the need to utilize the supply strategically – to build organization, generate employment and make money.

In the example of finding community and giving this place, we recognized the catalyst properties of bus stops and formed a mental image of their potential based on precedent. There was, in that sense, a structure by design, a certain predictability about means and ends and yet, still, an indeterminacy about the precise form each would take. We worked somewhere between knowing and not knowing what might happen. We provided ample opportunity for the results of our first decisions – routing the bus line, positioning the bus stop – to tell us something about subsequent actions that may induce a change of mind, a change in direction or even a change of objective. We avoided pre-emptive answers, in this case to community, and instead facilitated its emergence. We sought to understand systems, networks, people, place, politics and resources which naturally produce community, in all its possible forms, and which will need progressive cultivation, spatially, financially, socially and even politically. We see in this way of working, a kind of practice that does not rely for its effectiveness on certainties or complete information. Nor do we rely on the usual preponderance of survey and analysis – the kind of ethnographic and reductionist surveys that tell us, for example, that people need 810 millimetres of space for polishing shoes, 150 millimetres of office space for telling stories or 4100-millimetre-wide pathways for horses and carts. Whilst we do need good understanding of how and why things work they way they do, we avoid the rational comprehensive world that demands intellectual capacities and sources of information as well as the kind of political and social stability which we rarely encounter in practice. We avoid detailed time charts, zoning diagrams or critical path analysis which demand the kind of expertise that would displace marginal entrepreneurs and ordinary people like Mela, Tandia and others, in favour of project officers, government bureaucrats, formal business and contractors drawn always from outside our place of work and sometimes even from other countries.

Instead, in practice, we need often to act spontaneously, to improvise and to build in small increments. First, spontaneity, as a quality of practice, is vital because most problems and opportunities appear and disappear in fairly random fashion and need to be dealt with or taken advantage of accordingly. Sometimes problems appear all at once and not according to predictable patterns. One therefore has to be selective, knowing that once one problem has been dealt with another will appear equally randomly. When you have run out of resources but not out of problems, you improvise – inventing rules, tasks and techniques as you go along. Improvisations then become a means of devising solutions to solve problems which cannot be predicted, a process full of inventive surprises that characterize the informal way in which many poor people gain employment, make money and build houses. Third, we need to build incrementally. Most settlements grow, consolidate, change and even disappear in a series of increments. Small businesses grow in a similar way, as do houses and communities. The questions is, to what extent are these changes inhibited or supported? And, having answered that question, what kind of intervention is appropriate at each of the various development stages?[11]

How do we turn a practical intervention, once decided, into strategic advantage? Our bus stop, for example, served to link design with emergence in order to meet the practical needs of now, and also began to serve the strategic demands of later. Because we had formulated clear objectives, widened the roads at their intersection to make space, carefully positioned the bus stop, giving all this a boundary, we had created a structure by design – in this case a spatial one. But we had done this in a way which would evolve into community – our strategic objective – with markets, meeting places and all the respective emergent social organization (the market cooperative, Tomi's delivery fleet and the community water board). What emerged was a community of place and, in it, all the other communities of practice around trading and servicing. At the same time, there was the more straightforward practical business of finding a place for buses to stop, the need to get fish to markets more easily, the demand to improve transportation to other parts of the city – to make it all more connected.

We find a similar combination of objectives when dealing with water, building houses or fighting fire. With water, there was the practical business of sizing the pipeline, planning the network and positioning the standpipes – a structure by design which would guarantee a clean and adequate supply. Then there was the emergent structure of organizations to manage and maintain the standpipes – again, a practical part of its evolution, encouraged, maybe even triggered, from outside. The tap attendants are one example. But in the process, both design and emergence lead us to think of much larger, more strategic objectives: to change behaviour in respect to water management, to empower women who, with children, we know are at the forefront of managing water and, in so doing, begin at least to disturb gender relations; to build organizations and encourage new partnerships which, when connected to others citywide, emerge maybe as a network, a part of the governance of water. The standpipe, like the bus stop, we recognize has emergent potential, a trigger for emergence. And in this process, we build both household and community assets – financial and social ones at least. With some training in organizational management, book-keeping and water maintenance, we also build human resource assets, and feed these into the larger network or alliance of community-based water trusts which, in partnership with state and private organizations, can help to improve the supply and management of water – and sometimes the other services and utilities as well.

Then there is the planning process itself and, in it, the place of practitioners. We will have witnessed that the process entails events (Patama's resettlement workshops, needs-based and rights-based workshops, planning the school garden and the water network) and, in between, all the street work and other work which took us forward. The community-based action planning workshops and events we had adopted served to offer an early insight into the organizational capabilities of community, the responsiveness of planners and government authorities to ideas, the appropriateness of standards, the potential for partnership and the resistance of those in charge to change or adapt. They explored the willingness of people and their local organizations to disturb their habits and routines. They are vehicles for learning and for identifying institutional capabilities and training needs, as much as for getting organized, getting going and solving problems.

The action planning workshops offer a basis with which to organize communities in ways to lobby city authorities for strategic city-level change. In this way, action planning serves important strategic functions which can influence policy and ensure local-level participation in the governance of cities. Neighbourhood organizations and community groups, according to O'Gorman, can 'carry their development beyond the bridges, schools, cottage industries or day-care centre' through a variety of mediums (newspapers and television, popular movements and political negotiations) and so influence or help formulate public policy.

The rationality of action planning, the workshop, street work and plan-making lies in the proposition that once sufficient work is done at the neighbourhood level, pressure begins to build up to act at city level and emergence begins to take place.

There will be two important differences to conventional planning, if we are to pay more than just lip service to this rationality. The diagrams on the next page illustrate first, that we will need to reverse the order of work and, in so doing, create more synergy and strengthen the linkage between practical ground-level work and the more strategic business of policy development and structure planning. It is about finding that balance between the structures we must design (strategic) and those that must emerge (practical, local), working with both the elite of city authorities and the pluralism of the grassroots – not either/or. Second, as outsiders working as we must with local counterparts both on the ground (NGOs, CBOs, local authorities, private entrepreneurs), and with national-level or urban-level partners (local authorities, national government and national-level private enterprise) we must increasingly move our territory of operation outside of these individual realms and place our practice firmly in between.

In the first case (Diagram B), convention has it that when planning starts it begins with making policy – for shelter, for example, or employment. We assume that if we can make good policy, then good programmes will somehow follow. We will be told that these policies reflect local need – sometimes they do, many times they don't. We proceed to design the larger order of structure first into which projects must fit, denying all the novelty we have discovered in community. The process is top-down. The relationship between the top and the bottom is awkward at best and sometimes is in stark and open conflict. All of this is reinforced by the planning process itself. We set objectives and priorities based on convention which planning deems necessary or desirable, or both, in the national or even global interest. We then embark on lengthy consultations (sometimes) and data-hungry surveys (always) designed (most

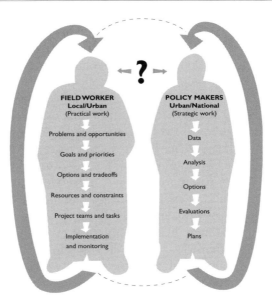

Diagram B *Conventional planning*

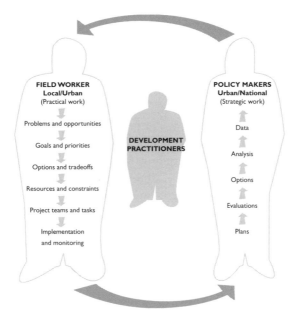

Diagram C *Action planning*

times) to get the answers we want to questions that we have set. It is a process designed to consolidate our position, to get what we believe to be right or desirable, perhaps with concessions. The data and information we get is then analysed (by us) which helps us set targets for housing supply and quality, for transportation, schools, jobs and the rest. It helps us argue *our* case to local groups rather than the other way round. Implicit already in all this analysis will be values and ethics embodied in standards and other criteria that will guide our search for viable policy options which will shape projects and programmes. These will be evaluated against a range of pre-agreed criteria, some drawn from our experience elsewhere and some to match internationally agreed goals for sustainability, reducing poverty or promoting rights. All will be legitimate and may also include an assessment of costs, political expediency, environmental appropriateness, social acceptability, institutional capacity, technological viability and so on. Finally, and some years down the line, a plan will be drawn up according to technical, political and sometimes ethical rationalities, but where, often, 'each rationality [will] seek to assert itself and win assent from others as to the priority of its goals and approach'.[12] This will be reflected in all the wrangling and negotiations to get it approved.

Attached to all this may be a spatial plan (the one with coloured bits all over it designating where you will play, work, live and shop) and also details of cost schedules, implementing partners, timetables for detailed design, implementation and management, ways to get the community to participate, or to win their approval. Sometimes there will be a risk assessment done, detailing some of the likely hurdles one might encounter which, in turn, will demand some contingency planning to mitigate risks. The risk assessment, the contingency plans and the time it has taken so far will have already invalidated the early data and will have raised further issues which need exploration. This will likely demand more surveys and data gathering to ensure the legitimacy and viability of the plan. The cycle of planning will repeat – it may not take so long this time round, some months not years, with more analysis which will reveal new options that will be evaluated again, and so on. Sometimes, of course, the plan will not have a practical purpose at all. It will be there for political expediency. It may lead to a proclamation for signature by the legislature or to be voted upon at the next UN cities conference or the like. But assuming it does have a practical purpose, then somewhere along the way a few projects will have got started – some housing will have been built, a road, a clinic, an upgrading project or two or an outmoded sites and services project – but not enough to make a real difference because, by the time you've done all the planning and thinking, you will have probably run out of money anyway for the doing. In any case, in the time it has all taken, the government will have changed, the international focus will have moved on to some other new agenda of priorities, the ceasefire amongst warring factions will have been called off and your favourite mayor will have moved on or been displaced. And probably, in the time it has all taken, the problems on the ground will have changed or disappeared or been managed by local people in their desperation, and other problems will have appeared. Local problems and issues will, therefore, be reshuffled and redefined to fit the strategic plan which, by this time, will be too expensive or too difficult to change. And the consultants will have long departed, leaving shelves of reports and plans that other consultants will now have to interpret before they can be made practical – which will, of course, need more study.

If we now turn our attention to the left-hand side of Diagram B, we will find the grassroots brigade, the insiders doing it all with community, championing the cause of bottom-up, in conflict persistently with the planners and the authorities. They will follow well-tried routines, applying to their work and process the latest in Planning For Real, Community Action Planning or PRA – beginning with problems and opportunities and leading to projects and programmes, getting something started quickly and visibly with each step leading to the next. They also are likely to lock themselves into their own loop of events, rarely venturing far into the strategic realm of planning except as activists to lobby and advocate. They will be long on process and short on product, despite the demand from most of the poor people, for the opposite. Because of this, community action planners have attracted legitimate critique: lots of good isolated projects and programmes but it never seems to add up to much, citywide. It never tackles the root cause of issues – always fire-fighting, despite the rhetoric. And because their heads are stuck in the ground whilst the strategists have theirs in the clouds, there won't be much learning from one to the other.

Moving in opposite directions, as both realms often do, leads to conflict when it comes to implementation – conflicts of interests, objectives, values and rationalities and even timetables. The result is a bad fit between policy and projects, if there is a fit at all, with a loss in trust and momentum. What we get is the kind of competitive environment in which those with the loudest voice or political clout always win – it is set up this way!

Instead, Diagram C presents an alternative. We have seen it work in practice, in our case study. It offers a different process and, at the same time, consolidates the role of the outsider as a catalyst, mediator, facilitator or enabler.

First, we avoid the unhelpful designation of good guys and bad guys because, tough as it is, we need both. We accept the legitimacy and importance of both realms of work in community and in government (and later, maybe, with global institutions and organizations) with their respective private-sector partners and look for ways of integrating their goals and aspirations. We do this first by reversing the order of work on the right-hand side of the diagram and feed the loop of policy planning with issues, problems, opportunities and priorities derived from the ground. We do this with the confidence that the 'projects loop' will have already involved all parties coming to terms with their sameness and differences and on the assumption that the bigger picture, the large order of plan or policy, if it is to serve the interests and needs of people, will derive from all the small and successful initiatives going on in the community. And so, working with local counterparts, starting small and starting where it counts, we build up the larger plan for social enterprise and good governance based on new forms of mutual engagement, a network of community-based partners in water or solid waste management, a new policy on shelter, a revised policy of land tenure, a spatial structure plan for infrastructure development. These larger plans will certainly need evaluation, on the basis of which options for implementation will appear and which will need analysis. This analysis will tell us something about gaps in our knowledge, an assessment of, and better understanding of, what impacts we are likely to achieve, what harm it might do

– which may lead us to more targeted data searches or surveys that will better inform our planning about local problems, opportunities and local risks and that, in turn, may demand revisiting our goals and priorities and so on. The process is cyclical and is more likely to lead us to a policy environment which is at once connected to issues on the ground and which facilitates emergence, which is enabling. It provides a framework of standards, legal structures and partnerships for mutualization and puts into practice the idea of network governance, which we defined earlier.

Second, and in all this, we find practice positioned again in the middle ground of the larger cycle which, by differentiation from either the field workers or city planners, enables practice to link both and to become developmental. In this mediating position – linking the practical and strategic world, the small scale with the large scale, public authorities with community and small enterprises with larger formal ones – we are more able to take advantage of our outside position by disturbing both realms of organization in the interest of change, to build networks and to feed necessary resources of information and good practice, as needed, to each and, so doing, to improve the governance of cities.

11

GOVERNANCE AND NETWORKS: ORGANIZING FROM INSIDE OUT

Dimensions and levels and scales – how to keep your feet on the ground and a seat at the table.

We have come to recognize the importance of emergence theory, of the relationship between designed structures and emergent ones, in reshaping our thoughts also on governance. We have begun to invent novel forms or civic engagement where government cooperates with, rather than serves, its citizens, moving from provider to enabler, much as it has learnt to do with the market. New forms of mutual engagement are emerging everywhere, based on participation and social entrepreneurship which is finding its way into the body politic of governance. Turnbull calls this 'Network Governance', an inside-out structure of social organizations and enterprises held together by well-connected and well-networked systems rather than command and control hierarchies or power elites analogous to organic systems and our earlier example of the slime mould.

> *The central question in the debate is: who governs the city? Is it a power elite in corporate boardrooms, or an executive-centred coalition in city hall, or warring sovereignties, or political machines, or public unions, or possibly even organized crime? Academic detectives have shown an almost insatiable appetite for finding new and seemingly better answers to this mystery. Nevertheless, two main positions exist: one is the power elite conception... the other is the pluralist conception.*[13]

Turnbull and others advocate a strong relationship between both in what he and Ed Mayo call Network Governance and Mutualization. Once again, it is not either/or:

Network organizations have much to offer society... Designed properly, they will allow us to replace economic forces and market competition with social forces and political competition. They will harness the private self-interest of executives to the public good. They will improve the self-regulation of organizations and, in the process, re-energize democracy. Inclusive 'stakeholder constituencies' will replace ruling elites and alienating command and centre hierarchies. Currently, we seem to face a choice between state-run enterprise or state regulation, or privatized and public interest companies. Stakeholder governance provides an alternative.[14]

An impassioned appeal indeed, but we see examples of this kind of social enterprise and good governance emerging everywhere: community contracts with waste pickers in Karachi; mutual management of water supply in Ethiopia; or the waste recycling enterprise in Brazil, Sri Lanka, Thailand and the Philippines.

In our own example, Mela's recycling centre, Tandia's green enterprise and all the other community-based initiatives citywide are all forms of interconnected or potentially connectable social enterprise, building networks which are socially inclusive and which adopt a long-term business plan rather than rely on short-term project funding. It is an organic collectivity which views Mela, Tandia, Tomi and organizations like the green enterprise and the recycling centre as people who may lack a global perspective but whose collective actions become 'a natural part of the effort at social reconstruction'[15] and an effective way of managing cities. 'These acts of association', said Edwards 'have power because they release social energy, meaning the willingness to act from one's ideals and moral conclusions – a desire to serve the community or a commitment to common interests. This is the energy that powers civil society across the globe in its encounter with the state and markets...'. They provide services which otherwise would not be available and 'enable local people to develop skills, self-confidence, business experience and employability'.[16] These acts of association rebuild commitment to wider society and, as we have seen, re-engage people as citizens. Under these circumstances, people and organizations – individually and collectively – are brought together in new relationships where the state is 're-imagined as democratic guarantor, regulating without interference, drawing out lessons through auditing participatory programmes, transferring knowledge and know-how, working as partners toward mutualization – that state of common ownership where public services and community enterprise are governed and run by its members'.[17]

These two recurring themes, partnership and mutualization, are at the heart of governance and underpin much of the recent, some say neo-liberal, thinking on participation. Like community, partnership is another one of those motherhood words incorporating everything good and desirable – mutual trust, respect, accountability, transparency, shared values, shared objectives and the mutual pursuit of ends and means. Instead, in practice and in that triadic relationship between the state, the market and community which underpins governance, we find mistrust, mutual disrespect, self-interest, conflicting objectives, corruption and unequal power relations. Brinkerhoff gives us an idealized summary:

> *Partnership is a dynamic relationship among diverse actors, based on mutually agreed objectives, pursued through a shared understanding of the most rational division of labour based on the respective comparative advantages of each partner. This relationship results in mutual influence, with a careful balance between synergy and respective autonomy which incorporates mutual respect, equal participation in decision making, mutual accountability, and transparency.*[18]

Or: each party doing what each does best for mutual gain.

From our earlier discussions on building respect, and throughout, mutuality recurs as fundamental to our work. It involves finding that balance between giving and taking, of making your presence felt as a partner by engaging in work and, equally sometimes, by holding back. 'Mutuality means that all partners have an opportunity to influence their shared objectives, processes, outcomes and evaluation... Mutuality refers to mutual dependence and entails respective rights and responsibilities of each actor to the others. These rights and responsibilities seek to maximize benefits for each party, subject to limits posed by the expediency of meeting joint objectives.'[19]

What we need for governance is to define afresh that triadic relationship between the state, the market and the community and then set out for each roles, responsibilities, duties and obligations.

Furthermore, it all has to be thought through in relation to the different forms of community identified earlier and then, at least, at three levels: the local, the national and the global.

If we recall the presentation in Bangkok, the one on governance, we will have seen displayed on PowerPoint a simple, idealized diagram (Diagram D) showing each of our three partner types abstracted into bubbles, equally sized, well linked, well harmonized and static in terms of power sharing, value sharing and the rest. Useful conceptually, I had thought at the time, but not very helpful in practice. For one thing, we know that power sharing is not equal. Indeed, we have seen how each of the principal conglomerates can become dominant, even malignant, and where linkages are often weak and sometimes non-existent and where relationships are dynamic not static. 'The relationship between national and local government, poor residents and cities, and other stakeholders are characterized by uneven distribution of power', said Carole Rakodi. 'Not only is their bargaining power unequal, but also their capacity to negotiate is determined by status, skills, expertise and experience which vary. Complex power relations are compounded by a donor and donor-recruited consultants.'[20]

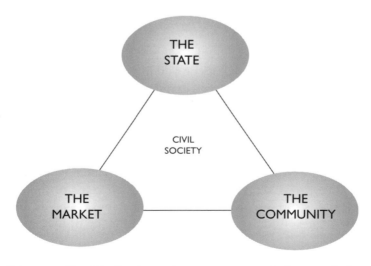

Diagram D   *Idealized: equal powers, symmetrical, strong links, consolidated*

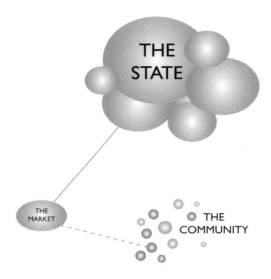

Diagram E   *Reality: unequal powers, unsymmetrical, weak links, fragmented*

A less idealized, more realistic configuration might look something like Diagram E – which is diagrammatically more representative of our starting point in our case examples.

For another thing, the terms 'state', 'market' and 'community' – like 'public' and 'private', 'formal' and 'informal' – collect bundles of differential vested interests into groupings, which in practice is unhelpful. We need to know the constituency of the entity we are dealing with and then position ourselves as practitioners accordingly. Diagram F, still idealized in its geometry, illustrates.

At the local level, and representing the state, we find local government with its various institutions which manage land, shelter, services and utilities. Its ability to govern will be heavily dependent on its institutional capacity and its status politically and financially with respect to its central government partners. The market will comprise small private enterprise, formal and informal; the community may well be made up of each of the five types of community: interest, practice, culture, resistance and place. Each will vary in its relationship to the state and, indeed, to the market.

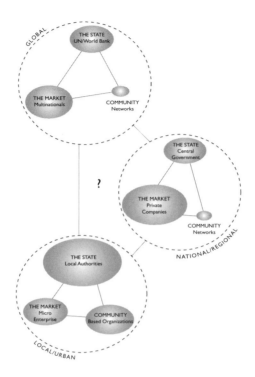

Diagram F   *Global governance*

The question here, and in respect to all other levels – national and global – is: what kind of partnership or mutual engagement might there be between the state, for example, and a community of resistance? And how will this be different, qualitatively in terms of duties and obligations, to its relationship to other types of community? At the national level, we find the institutions of central government working often with national-level private enterprises, managing infrastructure, transportation, utilities, health and education. Their ability to govern and meet their objectives and pledges will, in turn, likely be dependent on global institutions and the extent to which they are tied to the turbulent forces of globalization – financial markets, trade, environmental regulations and debt servicing. Community, at this level, includes networks of local organizations that may have formally or informally federated in order to achieve a common purpose and win a stake in the politics of state. Again, there will be networks of communities of resistance, interest, practice and the like. What, then, is their relationship and what potential is there for partnership between actors at this level? Are these institutions of government able or willing to partner with communities of resistance in search of meaning and identity?

At the global level there will be global institutions, the various UN organizations, the World Bank and IMF, the WTO, WHO and OECD countries and others in the aid business – EU, USAID, DfID for example. Their agendas are interpretable depending largely on whether you belong to those who are doom-mongers or those whose business it is to keep hope alive. They will often be in alliance with, or indeed in direct partnership with, the multinationals who they will have encouraged to engage in development, who will have, in any case, seen it all to be profitable. Their corporate social responsibility will demand they engage, even benefit, local communities. Community representation at this global level is weak. But networks are emerging, facilitated by the Information Technology Revolution and what Castell calls the 'network society'.[21] Whilst this goes beyond community networking and often engages criminal cartels there is, nevertheless, a groundswell of grassroots organizing and activism in response to the forces of globalization but which have yet to be engaged by international institutions or markets. The international forum on collaboration, which is a non-profit organization, that provided 'the philosophical background for the worldwide coalition of grassroots organizations that successfully blocked the meeting of the WTO in Seattle and made its opposition to the WTO's policies and autocratic regime known to the world' is an example.[22] There are consumer groups, too, mobilizing around free trade or GM crops with newly found corporate partners.

Diagram F raises four further questions: first we have come to understand good governance at the local level and maybe at the national level as well. But what is good governance at the global level? What does it mean to bring back the state and make it more accountable in the fourth dimension between local, national and global levels? Martin Khor says that '...there has to be a much more favourable international environment, starting with the democratization of international relations and institutions, so that the South can have an active role in decision making. The developing countries should have more rights in participation, in decision-making processes, in the IMF, World Bank and WTO which should also be made accountable to the public and to local and poor communities'.[23] This is indeed also George Monbiot's theme, in his book *The Age of Consent*. In it he cites the deeply undemocratic processes of the IMF and the World Bank, dominated as they are by the G8 nations who hold some 49 per cent of the votes and of the WTO. The USA alone holds some 17 per cent of the votes and can veto any resolution which does not fit its own needs.[24]

Second, what does the concept of mutualization and partnership mean when we consider partnerships between, say, the state and the market but at different levels? For example, between community and networks at the local, national and global level; or indeed between small entrepreneurs and informal traders at the local level, with private or market partners at the national level and corporations at the global level? Are there linkages and relationships that have yet to be explored in the interests of governance, global governance in the fourth dimension and, if so, what qualitative form are they likely to take?

Third, and here we must decide the places of practice, where do NGOs typically operate and where should they operate? Many we have seen work with community at the local level. Others work with community at the national and even global level. Some also work in the first dimension and others in the second, even nowadays the third. But are they prepared to step into the global middle ground – the fourth dimension where the stickiest problems lie – mediating between levels and not just partners, giving an added voice at the global round table to the millions of still poor and vulnerable?

'…NGOs have been increasingly effective in bringing the voice of civil society to the global arena', says Edwards. Three types of involvement have become especially important: (1) changing the language of debates and bringing on board the social or human dimension; (2) negotiating the detail of regimes, for example over landmines; (3) monitoring and enforcing global agreements. 'The

NGO working group on the World Bank meets the Bank's Board of Directors once a year... while the various NGO consultative groups in the UN system meet more often...'.

'"James Wolfson has bought priceless support from shareholder governments by opening the doors of the World Bank to Oxfam and other well-known campaigners on debt, health and education.' Edwards goes on to say: 'Globalization requires both governments and NGOs to link different levels of their activities together – local, national, regional and global'.[25]

And finally, where do practitioners sit? Their choice of partner level and dimension will decide the course of their careers. Again, much of practice, at least amongst those who advocate the cause of enablement and community participation, is commonly based at the local level. Most of the participatory networks and techniques – much of PRA, RRA and CAP – have focused on improving practice working with community. Some opt to work with local government and yet others – the small enterprise brigade – work with the informal and formal market at the local level. Some, the policy planners, institution builders and government administration experts, will work with central government administrations – some with national or regional community networks (ACHR, Peoples Dialogue, Bangladesh Rural Advancement Committee (BRAC) – some even with national enterprises. Others opt for UN organizations, for the new socially responsible corporates and their newly established foundations – Shell and Coca Cola, for example. Yet others, like the NGOs, indeed those who work for the NGOs nationally and globally, will operate between levels, often working with the state, the market or the community. Again, what of the fourth dimension? And, in respect to each of these realms of practice, what do we need in skills and competencies, and do they differ from level to level or dimension to dimension? What commitment to ethics, that agenda 'predicated not on accepting things as they are, but on struggling to make them what they ought to be: to create new possibilities in the supreme moral imperative'?[26] Opening doors, removing constraints, working somewhere between Goulet's three rationales of development – the technical, political and ethical[27] – each with its own view of the world and its own goals, and all three applied cyclically, locally, nationally and globally.

12

RIGOUR AND RELEVANCE:
IT CAN BE BOTH

*How practice doesn't exactly make perfect, but then neither does theory,
and in practice, practice teaches a lot better than teaching.*

If we were to sum up the demands placed on practice in the setting and circumstance of Part 2 in this book and give a definition, it might read as follows:

> *practice – the art of making things possible, of expanding the boundaries of understanding and possibility in ways which make a tangible difference for now and for later, making expert knowledge more widely accessible, turning it all into common sense and common sense into experts' sense, coupling knowledge with power (Shovkry), creating opportunities for discovery (Chambers), finding creative ways of making one plus one add up to three or even more.*

Practice is about opening doors, removing barriers to knowledge and learning, finding partners and new forms of partnership, building networks, negotiating priorities, opening lines of communication and searching for patterns. It means designing structures – both spatial and organizational – and facilitating the emergence of others, balancing dualities that at first seem to cancel each other out – between freedom and order, stability and creativity, practical and strategic work, the needs of large organizations and those of small ones, top and bottom, public and private. And all this in a world which is inherently unequal and unstable locally, nationally and globally – working with all levels, working in between levels, all competing for power and resources.

What we need, in this complex environment, is a kind of professional artistry which enables us to improvise and be informed, working somewhere between order and chaos, making what we can out of what we can get, making plans without too much planning, making most of it up as we go along, a creative process of trial and error informed with experience and theory. It is the kind of theory we find in practice, called praxis, derived from the Greek word *theoria* meaning contemplation, spectacle and material conception rooted in sight. 'Good theory helps us explain what is happening in real life. Theory does not mean abstraction.'[28]

Professional artistry demands both skill and wisdom. It is the kind of wisdom which 'brings unity out of multiplicity after facing contradiction and complicity'[29] and which enables us 'to think and act utilizing knowledge, experience, understanding, common sense and insight'.[30]

But what does it take to become skilful and wise? What skills and knowledge do we need and how best are these acquired? How do we educate the intellect and, also, the heart and spirit of the mind? What educational environment for learning does this demand? How should it be internationalized? And, in any case, what does it mean when we say we want to be international in a global world? And once we know, as teachers and learning institutions, how best can we reflect this knowledge and understanding in pedagogy and curricula?

In the old days, it all seemed much more straightforward. Teaching practice internationally meant going overseas, doing field work abroad, selecting a site in some faraway place which you could visit on a study trip during the cold and dark days of January. Schools built their reputations by specializing in overseas work, which meant mostly dealing with conditions of climate and culture at odds with your own, and with resources that were always hopelessly inadequate. In practice, you sometimes spent long stretches of time in countries which were too hot, too cold or just too far away. The further away you went and worked, the more international you were thought to be, the easier it was to try things out at other peoples' expense, to make mistakes without recourse. At home and for schools, being international, if it mattered at all, had much to do with how many overseas students you could attract, how many British Council link programmes, Erasmus or Socrates students (programmes established by the European Union to facilitate the exchange of students amongst universities), international visitors, staff exchange programmes and overseas funding. It meant familiarizing yourself with international law, standards available, technologies, codes of practice.

Whether at home or abroad, being international meant being intellectually and geographically 'away from home'. It meant dealing with other people's problems rather than your own. It gave you status and earned you money, which were the envy of colleagues and competitors. It was professionally empowering.

Inherent in the old-world notions of international practice are a complex set of assumptions – an ethos of practice still difficult to dislodge which guided our teaching and learning. These are assumptions about whose knowledge and expertise is best or more advanced about the universal value of what were Western-styled models, systems, building types and technologies which we associate with modernity; about the roles and responsibilities we assumed to be the mandate of professionals and the better off, about the nature of progress and about practice itself. We advanced toward a better future with the kind of certainty and conviction which only the ignorant or powerful can afford to assume about what we had to offer and where it was most needed.

When it came to teaching we followed the routine and rationale of serial thinking, and the reductionist science of Newtonian physics which says 'hey, the world out there is complicated and a mess – but look! Two or three laws reduce it all to an incredibly simple system'.[31] It was an organized simplicity which, in planning, followed the linear pattern of survey–analyse–plan (and later) implement. The principal mode of teaching was single disciplinary, preferring single-function projects – housing, schools, science museum or shopping malls. If they were planners or architects, their spatial plans would have been behaviourally deterministic and in compliance with the orthodoxy of the day, representing end-states – something you measure and preferably photograph. It was a process guided by goals you set out at the start, with targets, deadlines, indicators of achievement and exit strategies. Most students were taught in a climate dominated by idealized single or single-body clients, most of whom were on your side and well off. They were usually articulate, spoke the same language and were unthreatened by the professional elite.

For students and those starting out in practice, what they will have learned inside will be in stark contrast to what they need outside, to be effective. This gap between classroom and field presents them with hard choices. On the one hand a commitment to social and maybe political ideals; on the other a commitment to careers and your status as a professional. The result is that even the most conscientious find themselves paralysed by guilt or ambition. Those who work in development find themselves voluntarily or otherwise discarding their disciplinary allegiance, and those who chase careers find themselves often without political purpose or social relevance.[32]

In the old days, it was all arguably easier and more straightforward. We did not, for example, have to struggle with the meaning of words like 'sustainability', 'empowerment', 'rights', 'enablement', 'participation' and all the ideals and ethics they embody. Poverty, community, conflict, livelihoods and civil society were largely the realms of others. Environmental issues had yet to find their way into the real politic of global institutions, of whom, in any case, there were few. There were, after all, no Rio Conferences and no Agenda 21s to worry about. Our schemes were largely free of political interference. They were 'in denial of political and ideological realities', which enabled us freely and creatively to get on with our architecture, planning or engineering. We seemed unwilling or unable to reflect on the appropriateness of our values, attitudes, ethics, roles and responsibilities in respect of the fast-changing climate of opinion about what it takes to be at once rigorous to our discipline and relevant to our public, visionary and practical, regionalist and international. We saw no need to search for a new professionalism, only to invent new forms with which to order an environment which we saw as disorganized, ugly, irrational and unauthorized. We were distrustful of the very processes which Jane Jacobs once described as the essence of city organization and life.[33]

For these new forms, techniques, building types and town plans we sought approbation not from our public who were largely bewildered by what was going on, but from our professional institutions and from like-minded colleagues. At times of uncertainty and when the competition got tough, we withdrew to the familiarity of the disciplinary core and in teaching to 'the comforts of departmental thinking'. We tended to our public (when we did at all) with benevolent paternalism – a constituency which interfered with our quest for art and excellence and whom we treated as consumers of, not partners to, our planning. We awarded each other prizes and professional acclaim for innovations to solve problems which we defined for ourselves. We gave star status to the new, the novel, the one-off, precisely because it set us apart from what we saw as mundane and won us distinction.

We wallowed in jargon and abstraction and in the kind of pedagogy which gave teaching primacy over learning, and teachers power over students. It encouraged all the habits which today we recognize as barriers to professional development: defensiveness, abstract talk, over-specialization, a pretence to certainty and consistency, control and predictability. Witness the following:

It was one of those Thursdays, more or less mid-term in architecture school, reserved for students to present their work for critique and discussion. In architecture school, we call these crits – formal, formidable and often intimidating occasions when the student must explain his work and defend his ideas in front of a panel of staff and other experts. The dignitaries assemble, each with reputations in their own right – a published book, a learned paper, an award-winning building, a loudmouth at staff meetings, a lifetime with the Overseas Development Administration. In front stands one student, in his final year of training. On the wall hung a collection of paper scraps with notes and diagrams and other doodles of his proposal for new housing in a poor part of Lima, Peru – an island site surrounded by roads. It was well drawn with bold gesture, a confident first stab at making explicit some deeply held belief about his site and his buildings. On the wall also are some photos copied from magazines of other housing projects he liked – in Germany, the UK and the USA – a site plan, a collage which resembled a tapestry, bits of string cloth and metal pieces mounted on plywood with dabs of paint here and there – his big idea, his abstract representation, which he was required to do. He had visited the site during his year out, some two years ago, but was not really sure it mattered. It was, after all, only a vehicle to his own ends of completing the course and getting his Diploma.

The student proceeded to explain his project and all its mystic symbols with a generous measure of 'you-knows' and 'kind-ofs' – an extended monologue of only partially comprehensible phrases to describe seemingly ordinary things. He knew how to impress his critics: a high-pressure space (a play area), spatially integrating elements (double doors between rooms), points of dynamic interaction (meeting rooms) and elements (walls) weaving their way at tangents, guiding circulation (corridors). His view of architectural education had taught him the value of abstraction, which hides as much as it reveals; to be fully understood is to be considered overly simplistic and lacking in thought. It would invite critique and opinion, which he knew is risky.

At the same time, his presentation had to craft another delicate balance between seemingly irreconcilable values and objectives: between his need to create a significant piece of architecture to satisfy his portfolio and in a language his critics (and later his examiners) would acknowledge, if not understand, and yet satisfy his own sense of social responsibility to issues and people he had seen and met in the Barriadas of Lima which, for now, must take second place. He would have to put this on hold for the time being – until later when he had done with academia.

After a while, partly in sympathy, partly out of curiosity and partly with impatience, our panel begin to nod in synchronized union, a non-committal gesture of recognition but giving nothing away other than wakefulness. Everyone begins to wonder what everyone else is thinking about and how they might position their responses: yes, I understand what he is saying and I like it (the student might, after all, be saying something of great worth and significance and I certainly want to be part of it); or, yes I understand and don't like it (and risk alienating myself from fellow critics whose head-nodding by now is not easily distinguishable from head-shaking); or, should I admit to being muddled (and risk instead that this would be a reflection on my own intellectual incapacity, rather than muddled thinking by our student). How was he going to respond without giving away too much about his architectural values, his allegiance to the international style and to all those 'isms' which colonize architecture: modernism or post-modernism, functionalism, deconstructivism and the rest?

Finally, and when it comes to comments, he decides to go for the safe option, something technical and uncontroversial. 'How do you get on to the site – how do you gain access, where is the entrance to the building?' he asks. The question is remarkable for its simplicity and directness, after all the conceptual gymnastics of the student's presentation. Our student, however, was mistrustful of its intent. His critic, he had been warned, was well known for his 'shooting from the hip' type questions, which he recognized as more threatening than inquisitive, designed to catch you out rather than to inform. The student weighs up whether or not this is a tripwire into a debate about functionalism or whether it is an honest enquiry about practical issues, like where you put cars, how you cross busy roads without risking your life and how you find your way into the building, given that its back was indistinguishable from its front.

The student becomes defensive and decides that nothing less than profundity would be acceptable. He launches into more abstraction. Entrance – fact or enigma? A celebration of leaving one world and entering another, symbolizing transgression between the world of habit and routine and that of feeling and calm – where light, materials and form impose upon the senses in unison and creative experience rather than utility. Entrance is history, a movement in time from one humble era where man is subservient to systems, to machines and power into a timeless world where freedom and self-perceptions dominate, where dreams can be lived and made real, where man can dominate technology and the anonymity of mass production. Unwittingly, our student reaches from his pile of ideological literature, which he had so far not dared feature in his presentation, to a well-thumbed copy of Fuller's *No More Second-hand God* and reads:

> *In the great quasi, 'democracies'*
> *So far as the general schemes of things is concerned*
> *The individual no longer exists.*
> *Mass production anticipates*
> *The individual selective functioning.*

In another section, he quotes from Fuller's Teleogic schedule for the universal requirements of a dwelling advantage:

Check list of the
Universal design requirements
Of a scientific dwelling facility
As a component of function
Of a new world encompassing, service industry –
Predesigned
Rather than haphazardly evolved
Which this avoids
A succession of short – circulated
Of overloaded burnouts
Of premature and incompetent
Attempts to exploit the ultimate
And most important phase of Industrialization,
To wit,
The direct application of highest potential of scientific advantage
Toward advancement of world living standards –
To be accomplished by inauguration of a
Comprehensive anticipatory technology
Scientifically informed of the
Probable variables and possible randoms. . .[34]

By the time our student had finished reading, the panel had become irritable with their own inability to decide how to critique the student's work and shuffled uneasily in their seats. 'But where do you put the cars?', repeated our panellist. It was then that the student realized he had made the wrong choice of response. His critics were, after all, seeking practical answers. He didn't really know where all the cars would go and gets pounced on. His tutor comes to the rescue and insists he takes heed of the critics' concerns in his next round of design iterations. Everyone concurs. The crit rambles on from issue to issue until everyone has had their say, has made their point – until time is up. Besides, it was nearly lunchtime and tummy rumbles were heard as frequently as questions about structure, enclosure, density and so on.

Mistrust, defensiveness, jargon and abstraction, intellectual competitiveness, an absence of social issues, disparate agendas: everyone congratulated themselves on how well it all went – no one was better off.

But times have changed and so, too, have pedagogy and the issues. New skills and knowledge and new wisdom have emerged.

What we need today is a multiplicity of settings and pedagogic form for learning and teaching, engaging with partners, values and cultures worldwide for mutual and open learning.

The skills we need seem to fall broadly into three groups: disciplinary skills, process skills and job-related skills. Disciplinary skills are more easy to teach, whether in nursing, education or engineering, because they are more easily codified with numbers, routines and language, and because they assume a core of operational processes which are explicit and technically able to be rationalized. They offer a context for learning which is relatively stable and easy to measure and model. In the still departmentalized world of academia, disciplinary skills and disciplinary knowledge and values are the basis around which curricula are designed and coursework organized. We set goals and learning objectives, and then set out a logical process by which they can be acquired and then measured. There is a large and inevitable measure of predictability about what you will learn, how you will learn it, in what order and on what timescale, so that you can become a competent and worthy architect, engineer, nurse, economist or anthropologist. In this sense, disciplinary teaching is good at educating the brain's intellect, whether in classroom or in field work. But disciplinary teaching and its skills core do not serve well the goals we have set out for architects, engineers and the like to become development practitioners. To be competent in practice and to be developmental we also need, as we have seen, both associative or parallel thinking (the brain's heart), learning by trial and error, dialoguing with experience, finding association between things, as our examples in Part 2 have demonstrated, and we need quantum thinking (the brain's spirit), questioning, holistic, moving the goal posts, challenging assumptions and breaking rules. These are process skills more than technical ones, which combine thinking with acting in pursuit of wisdom.

In the third case, we need job-related skills. In their recent investigations into the skills and competencies which emergency field workers themselves found useful, Raymond, McKay and MacLachlan concluded that there are a number of 'people skills' which improved job performance and which they grouped into five categories. Coping skills included a sense of humour, knowing one's own limitations, knowing how and when to turn off. Then there were relationship skills – being sensitive to the values and routines of other cultures, adapting your pace, taking advice not just giving it, openness to learning; communication skills included diplomacy and tact, negotiation, social skills, verbal and non-verbal competencies, probing without interfering, using ordinary language, developing presentation skills to suit a variety of complex settings and client groups. Under the category of analytical skills, we might include all the PRA repertoire of routine for interviewing, listening, looking and mapping, as well as the ability to evaluate impacts, including harm. Self skills include the ability to be assertive, adaptable, flexible, tolerant and to take initiative, working with opposites.[35]

All these kinds of skills we nurture and teach in a combination of field work, of simulated field work and classroom teaching, and then through lifelong learning through reflective work. In the field, we find all the ambiguities we have discussed so far, all the frustration. The lines between teacher and student become blurred as we confront clients (community leaders, NGOs, ordinary people) who become teachers; as we encourage horizontal learning between students and between community groups, between NGOs, and as we test old theories and experiment with new ones. In group work and in the field, we explore diplomacy, negotiation, assertiveness, flexibility and all the analytical skills which enable us to understand the structure of place as we make explicit the tacit knowledge of community. Students struggle with never enough time, always working through gatekeepers, the ethics of arrival in community and entry into homes. They develop a sense of their own worth in relation to colleagues amidst the frustrations of learning without contributing, of being outsiders, of raising expectations and not being able to follow through with one's proposal.

In field work, learning is self-ordered. You learn what you need as you go along and do what you need to do to learn. You discover your own strengths and weaknesses and your own realities. You learn to cope, to be disappointed, to temper your ideals maybe but never your aspirations. In the words of one student:

We believed we could produce something that would work and help change peoples' lives. Many of our discussions centred around convincing

each other that our plan would work because it was a good idea; we
believed in it; our community needed it. But if it's such a good idea, why
didn't someone else think of it before? Or, why aren't they doing it now?
Our attempts at brainstorming to generate new ideas were hampered
by the lack of time and by our inability to disentangle personalities from
ideas. In a hurry, we would seek immediate agreement, which may have
stifled our individual creativity. The big ideas we were looking for, the
ones that would change the world, didn't come; whether they exist or
not is another question. The challenge for our group then became how
to accept the mediocrity of an idea and figure out how to reform it into
a viable option.[36]

In contrast to the mess of field work, in the classroom life is more clinical, more structured and directed. Workshops, role play, lectures have clear learning objectives. Experience is ordered, and practice methods principled. There is time to reflect – to draw lessons, to build your own code of conduct, to develop your own understanding of what are often competing theories.

This progressive and lifelong learning cycle of field work and class work, of practising theory and theorizing about practice, of self-discovery and structured enquiry, enables us to be at once rigorous and relevant. It shifts the emphasis of learning 'from knowledge and wisdom to a form of enquiry in which what we do and what we are make as much as, or more than, what we know'.[37] It is a form of enquiry grounded in common sense.

Wisdom demands common sense – that unspoken context of tacit knowledge we pick up in field work that lies hidden in community and in all the other institutions, formal and informal, that manage cities and make things work. A great deal of artistry in practice, of the knowledge and skill we need to work effectively, is embedded in experience, not easily described or articulated. Academia denies this kind of knowledge, precisely because it is difficult to articulate, codify and teach but which is, we know, fundamental to associative learning – the brain's heart. To quote the much quoted Schon: '...although we sometimes think before acting, it is also true that in much of the spontaneous behaviour of skilful practice, we reveal a kind of knowing which does not stem from a prior intellectual operation'.[38] Instead, we draw on our sense of purpose and experience and feel our way intuitively and artistically.

'I learn this skill, but I can't articulate any rules by which I learnt it and usually I can't describe how I do it... We feel our skills, we do our skills, but we don't think or talk about them.'[39]

And yet we know that tacit knowledge, which is fundamental to learning, can be expanded in ways that transform it into explicit knowledge through social interaction and open learning. This difficult to explain context of practice is made explicit by reflection in group work. Students reflect on the tacit knowledge embedded in their experience or derived from the field and, by reflection, make it explicit in class work. In so doing, they turn common sense into expert sense and pass it on to others in the form of good theory, best principles and, later, better practice. It enhances our understanding of practice and, in particular, the implications of our actions. It enables us to act with the right intentions, but with an ability to judge justice or injustice when we intervene and disturb the order of place. It enables us to be ethical.

This cycle of doing and learning, learning and doing, acting and reflecting involves a kind of 'activist pedagogy' which is systemic to becoming skilful and wise. The purpose, then, of teaching, given this setting 'is fundamentally about creating the pedagogical, social and ethical conditions under which students agree to take charge of their own learning, individually and collectively', to create their own knowledge, much in the same way as later, in practice, we would expect people to take charge of their own development.

In this climate of reflective, open learning in education and in practice, information about the negative impacts of proposals is not withheld from other participants. Assumptions are tested publicly and negotiation about priorities, responsibilities and possible courses of action is conducted in open forum. The objective throughout is to learn about what is most likely to work and who is most likely to be affected and how, rather than to push through pet ideas or idealized solutions. Thus, in a reflective or open-learning contract between teachers and students 'the [student] does not agree to accept the [teacher's] authority, but to suspend disbelief in it. He agrees to join the [teacher] in inquiring into the situation for which the [student] seeks help...'.[40] This shared pattern of inquiry leads to a restructured understanding about needs, desires and goals, as well as about the nature of problems, the aspirations of people, the constraints imposed by culture, politics and those who hold power. It follows 'the Freirian concept of "Conscientization", calling for raising the self-reflected awareness of people (including [our students]) rather than educating or indoctrinating them, for giving them power to assert their "voice" and for stimulating their self-driven collective action to transform their "reality"...'.[41]

In teaching, as in practice, these converging and interdisciplinary worlds demand partnerships with people and institutions who can bring to the academic setting an agenda reflecting cultural, political, social and economic diversity. It involves partnership between institutions representing national interests and between students, researchers and teachers. What we seek is a convergence of interests which enable mutual and open learning around issues and problems of common concern, rather than to give primacy to one set of interests over others. Learning in partnership, like interdisciplinary work, enables each party to have their voice heard, to understand better their own problems and experiences, not just those of others. We do this by engaging and accommodating those who hold counterviews, whose culture, attitudes, traditions, rituals, values and ethics may be at odds with our own. In this way, we may better understand how and why those others see what they see the way they do, so that we can expand our knowledge of common issues and come to terms with our own ignorance. Open learning is about cultivating mutual respect, about building each other's capacity to learn and influence practice – to be catalysts for change in each other's world, not just our own. It is about the getting of wisdom and about being reflective in practice as a 'corrective to over-learning' in schools. It is about being rigorous and relevant – about becoming international and ethical and about contributing developmentally.

In all respects, we are bound to broaden our agenda of issues and engage partners from other disciplines and other worlds, vested interest groups and client bodies with whom we may not be familiar. Some see all this as watering down our core skills and competencies – an undermining of our need to differentiate ourselves from others, lowering our standards, putting the brakes on high fliers who want to get on without the inconvenience of issues that seem peripheral to planning, engineering, architecture or nursing. Others – those who stick rigidly to the security of disciplinary work – see all this 'in-between' work as neo-liberal talk, as a threat to disciplinary identity. To them, it smells of the middle ground, of compromise and fence-sitting, of a new breed of chameleon 'professionals' willing to go whichever way the market demands.

I see it as strengthening each practitioner's disciplinary role and professional competency by enabling each to join and influence the global discussion on matters today of profound social and practical importance – of becoming international in a global sense.

13

Playing Games – Serious Games

*Where working backwards can move you forwards more quickly,
and where not knowing can be liberating.*

In summary, I offer the following code of conduct based on my own experiences and those of others, for teaching and practice, and in no particular order of importance. Each is open and interpretable. Together, they can change the way we think and work and learn and teach.

Work Backwards, Move Forwards, Start Where You Can

We have already witnessed the importance of this idea in the planning process in Chapter 10, working to plan–analyse–survey in progressive cycles. We have also learned to accept that development is ongoing, not something we start. When we do intervene or are invited to disturb, we are in this sense a part of the development continuum. We join the process somewhere along the way and try to help it along with new ideas, new wisdoms, new technologies and new skills. We do this because development has been interrupted, not because it hasn't started.

But there is one further consideration with respect to working backwards, a nuance maybe but important nevertheless: start at the end. It represents that quantum mind, open and creative. It opens doors to new opportunities rather than assumes pre-emptive answers.

For serial thinkers, two and two equal four – always. The answer is finite and predictable. But what does four equal? My maths colleagues tell me that the answer is infinity. Reversing the order of question, starting with what you think at first is the end – the answer – opens up new opportunity and thought processes which are less easy to predict, especially in development. Take an example: convention has it that land plus credit, plus ownership, plus services and access to resources, plus minimum acceptable standards equals house. The answer, in terms of type, affordability, tenure and even style is more or less predictable, according to some average worked out in some housing department. But what does a house equal? The opportunities are immense in terms of both process and product, and are more qualitative: wellbeing, dignity, status, self-respect, security, entitlements, skills, employment, enterprise, privacy and so on. When we add the variable *here* and then *for you*, when we contextualize the question, it gives us a chance to ensure the answer itself is tailor-made to the specifics of place and people. The answer, in other words, will be different every time – it is open and even less certain. The same holds true for all other development initiatives – health, education, enterprise and the rest.

There is a desire as you move to become knowledgeable and more hungry for data – to know it all before you start. You can never know it all.

Recognize Your Own Ignorance

Recognize your own ignorance and take advantage of your naivety. Avoid the library, the resource centre, the Internet as first steps to finding out. They come later. Start in the field in your own mental library of experience and intuition, limited as this may be in the beginning. Not knowing can be an advantage. It leaves space to think creatively in search of alternatives. It can be liberating. And, if we accept that in today's climate of uncertainty and complexity, wisdom holds more value than knowledge in practice, then it follows that who we are, how we work, is more important than what we know. In any case, knowledge untested in 'sight' makes bad theory – it doesn't help you become skilful or wise.

Today's intelligent practitioners, however knowledgeable, are more like Plato's philosopher than Newton's scientist: people who stand somewhere between knowing and not knowing, or at least between what they know and can explain and what they know and can't. They will be suspended timelessly in a state of optimal ignorance – knowing just about enough to play the game well and make a difference. They will recognize that however much they know, they will never know enough to be certain about results; however much we may judge or predict, it will always wind up differently; whatever visions we hold, it will always change. 'In this regard', said Georg Simmel, 'we are all like chess players. If [we] did not know, to a certain extent what the consequences of a certain move would be, the game would be impossible; but it would also be impossible if this foresight extended indefinitely'.[42] In this case, there would be nothing left to discover!

The more I seem to know, the less I seem able to achieve because all that I can see are barriers to progress. Given this context, it is easy to find oneself saying 'can't' and then looking for something much less challenging and significant to do, just because you can, just because you need to get on, because time is running out. The result: lots may be done but little is achieved, not much is changed.

NEVER SAY CAN'T!

If you find yourself saying 'can't' you are probably on the wrong path. You have chosen a problem too complex to resolve for now – you are on the wrong rung on that ladder to achieving your purpose, you are looking at the problem the wrong way. You need to turn it all upside down and look at it all from a different angle, a different point of view – maybe not your own. This is where participation counts. It helps develop a different point of view, to generate ideas, as much as to be involved in the policies and power relations of bureaucracy and decision making. 'It's easy to think of violent objections to every idea. It's easy but unwise. It is unwise because that will stop the idea in its tracks before it has had a chance to stretch itself... It's easy to listen to an idea and say "why?". It is more exciting to listen and say "why not?".'[43] And those who say 'why', those who say 'can't' will bring all kinds of evidence to support their reasoning because they will be threatened, because they fear change, because they will lose power. Soon enough, evidence takes primacy over ideas. Nothing changes because evidence has never changed the world, ideas change worlds.

'Can't because', has to become 'can if', if we are to avoid paralysis given all the obstacles in the way of what we want to achieve. If you get stuck, jump – don't retrench. Reframe the problem, see it in another context. 'Reframing unlocks problems, like an unexpected move on (Simmel's) chessboard, it can give the whole situation a new look. It utilizes the right side of the brain (creative) to complement the more logical left side.'[44] It can be intuitive, based on some hunch, or it may be unlocked with a new word or metaphor or a different view of the world.

Looking at things upside down and inside out stimulates the imagination, that other ingredient of creative practice which got us going in the Introduction to this book.

LET YOUR IMAGINATION WANDER, REASON LATER

Step into the world of hyperthought, then think the unthinkable – it might lead you to worlds that at first you thought unimaginable. Imagination is as important as knowledge or skill when looking for ways of unlocking ideas to solve problems and expand their scale citywide or nationwide. We saw ample examples in our case work in Part 2 – the bus stop, the pickle jar, the waste pickers, the intermittent standpipe and all the innovations with partnerships and enterprise and organization and governance which we were able to imagine and then reason, which we were able to generate. Dream, because without dreams we won't find new worlds, we won't invent new futures. But dreams alone can also 'give wings to fools' unless they are grounded and tested, unless they are worked with and made real by people whose lives will be changed.

When Patama's community dreamed their new houses, they were confined by their own experiences – their dreams were too real. They were like Kakus' family of fish swimming around in their fish bowl with no sense of an outer world or, if they had, no means to get there. In his example, 'one of the fish suddenly takes a big leap that raises him above the surface of the water in his bowl. "Ah", he says, "look where I've come from". He sees the bowl and his fellow fish and the water from this further perspective and sees that he has come from a world of fish bowls and water. And now he also knows that there is larger world outside the fish bowl, a medium in which to move other than water'.[45]

Practice, and in particular practitioners who are 'outsiders', can reveal these other worlds and, in so doing, can disturb people into reconstructing their situation, bringing them to a new awareness and, therefore, power that increases their freedom – which is what development is about.

BE REFLECTIVE

Whether in practice or when learning, be reflective, rediscover the art of wasting time creatively, because people in a rush don't stop to think about what they have learnt and what it means: why did I do that or ask that question? What will be the impact of this or that – who will be disadvantaged, who will get hurt and who will benefit? Move fast, therefore, but don't rush. There is an old saying that goes: 'If you haven't got time, you should have come yesterday'. Recognize that it takes time to know. Avoid deadlines. Follow your intuition, explore your hunches. Until you know the 'why' of things, you will not have learnt enough to change much. Don't think too much, therefore, before you start working; and don't work too much before you stop and start to reflect: to raise new questions or reframe old ones, to review the theories that got you started in the first place and framed your first intervention, for participatory work, good governance, sustainability, shelter, for education and for development – to invent new questions or adapt old ones and test them on site, in sight, and with more reflection become skilled and wise. This is the 'wheel of learning' that Handy talked about in his book *The Age of Unreason*. Thought and action go hand-in-hand – obvious!

> *Physically inactive thought (mistrusted by Nietzsche) and mentally inactive action (mistrusted by sensible people) are diseases of civilized people. Physical action in affluent civilization today is reserved for brutalities, chores and play. Mental action is practised chiefly by the physically inactive.*[46]

Schon also talks of thought and action as two sides of the same coin, of 'thinking about doing something while doing it'. He argues that much reflection in action hinges on making mistakes and on open learning. We want to reflect on things that go well or badly in order to apply continuously corrective measures as we go, or to modify the norms and methods of enquiry and action for next time. Reflective practice qualifies or disqualifies the assumptions we make and the value we apply when defining problems, setting priorities or evaluating alternatives before we intervene. It tells us about the appropriateness of the norms and standards we apply and take for granted, the process we adopt, patterns of behaviour we assume to be current or acceptable, or otherwise, about our attitudes and judgement. Reflection nurtures wisdom and is a corrective to over-learning in schools.

Embrace Serendipity

Schon also argues that reflection in action hinges on surprise and on chance. It follows that practice should embrace serendipity and search out chance with purpose. Don't try to sort out the mess and ambiguity – engage with it. Give chance a chance. Be prepared to get muddled because you cannot possibly hold it all in your head. Recognize that getting muddled is a prelude to creative work. Encourage random encounters. There is an old Arabic saying about tying your camel: position yourself with purpose (tie your camel) and then let circumstances guide you along.

Our stumbling into Tandia's pickle jar, the school's demise with its art building, our encounter with its headteacher, were all by chance. But it was our purpose that led us to recognize their value and our theories which helped shaped them into plans. Our bus stop was purposeful and by design – cultivating chance and random encounter that led to a multiplicity of opportunities for entrepreneurship and to the emergence of community in place and to the formation of other and sometimes novel organizations.

When things are complex, when we know we don't know enough to be certain, we play with chance. We simulate, we model or create other forms of representations of social, spatial or other relationships which enable us to get information and plan and test ideas with others. We play games – serious games, the kind with a well-thought-out purpose that help us explore and become knowledgeable, that help us learn and teach and not the kind you win.

'In dreams begin responsibility', said the poet, and in games begin realities.[47] In teaching and in group work, we socialize differences around a particular and real problem set in order to see how each individual sees what they see, and why they see it the way they do. It helps us to see it the way they do. It helps us to see it all from outside our own fish bowl. We may develop a new point of view and test a new idea. What if we try this or that? We may use picture analysis to highlight differences in values and perception and show that differences need not be threatening. In role play, we build an awareness of the need and desire of people and organizations that may not be well represented in community. We may ask adults to role-play children or men to assume the role of women in order to build awareness of age, gender, disability, caste or class. In teaching, we may ask one group of students to play the role of the World Bank, another an international NGO, another a community-based organization. We explore the often conflicting values and interests and test out ways of accommodating these differences. We may use trust walks to build collaboration between disparate groups. Much of this kind of activity is inherent in many of today's participatory planning work – in our early action planning workshops, in Patama's resettlement process, in PRA or in planning for real.

Whatever the game, all share a number of characteristics that differentiate game work from routine. In all cases, participants agree to play according to a given set of rules – a structure designed with purpose. They accept, therefore, a shared context for the work – a prelude already to planning; the outcome is never predetermined – it emerges in process; the process itself is fun. 'Serious games combine the analytic and questioning concentration of the scientific viewpoint with the intuitive freedom and rewards of imaginative artistic acts... In short, serious games offer us a rich field for a risk-free, active exploration of serious intellectual and social problems.'[48] They enable us to explore relationships between designed structures (rules) and emergent ones.

CHALLENGE CONSENSUS

In planning, convention has it that game work helps also build consensus. Challenge consensus or the search for some absolute truth that you can evidence with numbers, as you were taught to do in school. It takes too long to get there, it's risky. And once you do get consensus, if you do, you can't be sure it will all last because things will change and a new power elite will emerge. Consensus, we know, is at the heart of participatory work. With it, we attempt to converge the interests and polarities amongst communities of interest, cultural, practice or place, so that we can minimize conflict, sort out our differences, define our common objectives, set our priorities. We try to reduce it all to something manageable. And yet, consensus – that state we reach when one party agrees to suspend its objections to an idea or proposal, agrees to disagree – is counterproductive and counter-creative in participatory work. It enables those who suspend their objection, who may be comfortable in their self-sufficiency and have no need of others, to step aside rather than get involved, to admit that whatever is on the table for discussion and decision will not change their lives that much, which often is precisely the purpose of planning. Consensus gains the passivity of people not their active participation. It is in this sense exclusionary and encourages independence rather than interdependence. It encourages non-participation.

In addition, the consensus view, often sought through market and user surveys, whilst informative, leads us sometimes to reduce complex phenomena into statistically averaged solutions or responses and to oversimplifications. That's fine for selling soap powder, but less so when we seek to reshuffle power or gender relations. Witness, for example, the standard floor plan or housing layout devised by local authorities in the old days of social housing: all were statistically reduced to fit the average anonymous family – the large one, the small one, the newly married one, the problem one. What do you do with a consensus view where 51 per cent of your public like to socialize as families and prefer dining/living rooms but 49 per cent don't?!

There is, however, another paradigm, a counterview which challenges the conventional wisdom of consensus planning and offers an alternative which is less comfortable in practice. Kaplan, for example, talks of the need to achieve that phase of interdependence 'when we no longer have to assert our individuality and independence against the world, because we are secure in ourselves and can achieve recognition of ourselves as separate, coupled simultaneously with the recognition of our inevitable dependence on others'. In this way, we move from a position of 'us and them' to one of 'we'. Kaplan says 'creativity and life are the result of tension between opposites... [where] harmony is attained not through resolution but through an attunement of opposite tensions... not through eradicating conflict but through dancing with conflict... We seek not compromise, but a living, continuously shifting balance by holding both polarities at once'.[49] In this way, and in practice, we move to conflict accommodation, not conflict resolution, recognizing that conflict and polarity are creative and necessary, together providing a wholeness of understanding, a unity of opposites, a better picture of where the truth lies and where the most reasonable responses will be.

All this gets us much closer to real life and gives us a better sense of what it might mean for practice. It means, for example, that many times we need to search out and work with individuals or individual groups rather than work with community – people who are prepared to work with us, a starter partner who can unlock doors or ideas, who may be good guys or bad guys, or sometimes in-between on our spectrum of ethics. It means ensuring the security of these individuals and groups in terms of rights, entitlement, legal status or safety so that they can move to interdependence with others and begin to participate in planning, in governance. It means sustaining the special and one-off whilst searching for the DNA of a larger collectivism that might one day emerge as an organization or become community. In so doing, we create the kind of social space that enables individuals and organizations to engage with each other in governance, more similar to Nakagaki's slime mould organism than any devised system of planning.

LOOK FOR MULTIPLIERS

Consensus planning, in summary, has a strong tendency to be reductive. It looks for common denominators. Instead, look for multipliers. Start small and start where it counts. Find a first and meaningful step.

In the old days, when it came to expanding supply – whether of goods, services, utilities or housing – and doing it equitably and effectively, we thought it best to centralize decision making and production so that resources could be concentrated and focused where need was greatest and, accordingly, properly managed. In this way, we could control quality and cost. Big organizations, we thought, were best at producing and managing large-scale systems. Good governance meant good government and lots of it (or none of it). Big was beautiful, small was difficult and not very efficient. If you wanted to solve problems like housing, you eliminated uncertainty (people), standardized your plans, your building components and your operations and it would all be more efficient to manage and mass produce. The fewer people and organizations involved, the easier and quicker it would all be. We now know the truth is somewhere between large organizations and small ones, centralized and decentralized, more government regulations and less government control. Big scale means lots and lots of organizations: some small, others not so small, networking, managing water, producing shelter, delivering services, working in partnerships and doing it all in lots of different ways according to all the differences in their circumstances. Variety, not standardization, is the measure of equity and efficiency. Governance, not government, is how to manage it all.

But we do need big organizations to think big and to think long term. Only the centre can think beyond the next annual report, can think in terms of global strategies that may link one or more of the autonomous parts or can devise global solutions to global problems, to champion local manifestations of global issues through global campaigns.[50] We do need organizations that can think globally and act globally.

Small may be beautiful but big is necessary and inevitable.

Looking for multipliers means looking for ways of connecting people, organizations and events, of seeing strategic opportunity in pickle jars, bus stops and rubbish cans and then going to scale. It means acting practically (locally, nationally and globally) and thinking strategically, and acting strategically (locally, nationally and globally) and thinking practically. It's not doing either/or but doing both, and doing it reflectively and progressively.

Lastly, recognize that we are in a business where failure is more common than success, however you want to measure it. Our successes, when we do achieve them, are limited victories, albeit vital ones in a world we know is rampant with inequity and injustice. The result is that we spend a significant amount of time riddled with guilt, commiserating, feeling remorseful and bad about ourselves. We find ourselves inadvertently or otherwise making promises or raising expectations which we cannot meet. We work for governments or organizations whose values we do not always share. We spend much time and care getting in, to provide assistance, or make proposals or projects, and much more time trying to get out (is it ethical, will we disturb it all too much and who invited us here in the first place?), and when we are out we think we should be in (for humanitarian relief, for assistance). At the same time, we see the appalling inequity of a world order designed to profit rich nations and punish poor ones with debt restructuring through structural adjustment programmes, market protectionism and unfair trade through subsidies to rich countries and tariffs on goods in poor ones – which perpetuate poverty, not eliminate it. In this global setting, as Chomsky once said, we are faced with more hard choices: 'Either – we acquiesce in global injustice and tyranny; or – we join the struggle for justice, democracy and freedom.'[51] Either way, we make sacrifices. In the first case we sacrifice, to some extent, our values and beliefs; in the second, we sacrifice careers. Either way, we suffer more guilt and remorse, more doubt, and so it goes on.

At best, this process of 'decent doubt' leads us to ask important questions, to reframe our problems, to be deliberate about change. It is good for learning, in the same way that making mistakes is good for learning. 'Getting it wrong is part of getting it right' said Charles Handy. But when we do get it wrong, when we do make mistakes or when we just can't do what we know is right, we need to recognize our own 'negative capacity', which is to have the 'capacity to live with mistakes and failures without being downhearted or dismayed'.[52]

'Unfortunately, self-hate or just a lack of self-regard is no way to start learning', said Handy, and certainly no way to practise. It forces us to become defensive and we resort to convention: we hide behind jargon or specializations, we oversimplify, we assimilate and, in so doing, we stop being creative or even effective. What we need is a 'proper selfishness – a responsible selfishness' which is a means of coping and learning and managing change – in which you are the centre with others looking out and not forever on some periphery, always looking in. Once again, it's not either/or. It is both.

Feel Good About Yourself

Feel good about yourself, don't be defensive. Don't patronize, either because you think you know best or because you think they do. Inspire, don't boast. 'Accept the limits of your own abilities without losing belief in yourself.'[53]

ACRONYMS

ACHR	Asian Coalition of Housing Rights
BRAC	Bangladesh Rural Advancement Committee
CAP	Community Action Planning
CBO	Community-based Organization
CENDEP	Centre for Development and Emergency Planning
DfID	Department for International Development
ECT	Ealing Community Transport
ESCOR	Economic and Social research Unit of the Department for International Development
EU	European Union
IMF	International Monetary Fund
ITC	Information Technology and Communication
NGO	Non-Government Organization
OECD	Organization for Economic Cooperation and Development
PRA	Participatory Rapid Appraisal
PSSHAK	Primary Systems Support Housing and Assembly Kits
RRA	Rapid Rural Appraisal
UN	United Nations
USAID	United States Agency for International Development
WHO	World Health Organization
WTO	World Trade Organization

Notes and References

Foreword

1 Hamdi, N and Goethert, R (1997) *Action Planning for Cities*. John Wiley & Sons, Chichester.
2 Ward, C (1976) 'Preface'. In Turner, J, *Housing by People: Towards Autonomy in Building Environments*. Marion Boyers, London.
3 Turner, J and Fichter, R (1972) *Freedom to Build*. Collier Macmillan, New York.
4 Hamdi, N (1991) *Housing Without Houses*. Van Nostrand, New York; Intermediate Technology Publications, London.

Introduction

1 Robertson, AF (1984) *People and the State*. Cambridge University Press, Cambridge.
2 Kaplan, A (1996) *The Development Practitioner's Handbook*. Pluto Press, London.
3 Johnson, S (2001) *Emergence: The Connected Lives of Ants, Brains, Cities and Software*. Allen Lane, The Penguin Press, London.
4 Ibid, p13.
5 Simmel, G (1971) *On Individuality and Social Forms*. The University of Chicago Press, Chicago IL, p137.
6 Zohar, D (1997) *Rewiring The Corporate Brain*. Berrett-Koehler, San Francisco CA, p50.
7 Berlin, I (1958) *Two Concepts of Liberty: An Inaugural Lecture Delivered Before the University of Oxford on 31 October 1958*. The Clarion Press, Oxford, p11.
8 Capra, F (2002) *The Hidden Connections: A Science For Sustainable Living*. Harper Collins, London, p106.
9 Johnson, S (2001) *Emergence: The Connected Lives of Ants, Brains, Cities and Software*. Allen Lane, The Penguin Press, London, p78.
10 Based on Gillespie, S (2002) 'Scaling up community driven development: an overview'. Unpublished working draft.

11 Edwards, M (2000) *NGO Rights and Responsibilities. A New Deal for Global Governance*. The Foreign Policy Centre in association with The National Council for Voluntary Organizations (NCVO), London, p10.

12 Zohar, D (1997) *Rewiring The Corporate Brain*. Berrett-Koehler, San Francisco CA, p38.

13 Jose Saramango quoted in *The Guardian Review*, 28 December 2002.

14 Jacobs, J (1961) *The Death and Life of Great American Cities*. Random House, New York.

15 Schon, DA (1983) *The Reflective Practitioner: How Professionals Think in Action*. Basic Books, New York.

16 Johnson, S (2001) *Emergence: The Connected Lives of Ants, Brains, Cities and Software*. Allen Lane, The Penguin Press, London, p1.

17 Harvey, D (1990) *The Condition of Post-modernity*. Basil Blackwell, Oxford.

18 Capra, F (2002) *The Hidden Connections, A Science For Sustainable Living*. Harper Collins, London, p106.

19 Mayo, E and Moore, H (2001) *The Mutual State*. The New Economics Foundation, London.

Part 1: The Setting

1 Manuel, A and Guadalupi, G (1999) *The Dictionary of Imaginary Places*. Bloomsbury, London.

2 Enge, E (2001) 'Poverty, inequality and aid: rhetoric and reality'. In Randell, T and German, T (eds) *The Realism of Aid: Reality Check 2001*, NPA, Norway.

3 See for example Fox, J (2001) *Chomsky and Globalization*. Icon Books, Cambridge.

4 Pettifor, A (2003) 'World economic outlook', *The Networker*, 23: 6.

5 Borger, J and Denny, C reporting in *The Guardian*, 21 March 2002.

6 Reported in *The Guardian*, 3 March 1985.

7 See *The Independent*, 10 September 2003, World Trade – Special Report.

8 See *The Independent*, 10 September 2003, World Trade – Special Report.

9 Capra, F (2002) *The Hidden Connections, A Science For Sustainable Living*. Harper Collins, London, p29.

10 Quoted in Haytor, T (1981) *The Creation of World Poverty*. Pluto Press, London, p83.

11   See *The Guardian*, 9 May 2003.

12   Capra, F (2002) *The Hidden Connections, A Science For Sustainable Living*. Harper Collins, London, p113.

13   'The lost decade'. *The Guardian*, 9 July 2003.

14   *Target 2015. Halving World Poverty in 15 Years*. Report Published by The Department for International Development (DfID) and Christian Aid, London.

15   Brown, P reporting in *The Guardian*, 23 May 2002.

16   Brown, P reporting in *The Guardian*, 23 May 2002.

17   Slim, H (2002) *By What Authority? The Legitimacy and Accountability of Non-governmental Organizations*. Background Paper for the Annual Meeting of the International Council on Human Rights Policy, Geneva, 10–13 January 2002.

18   Edwards, M (2000) *NGO Rights and Responsibilities. A New Deal for Global Governance*. The Foreign Policy Centre in association with The National Council for Voluntary Organizations (NCVO), London, pp9–15.

19   Hamdi, N (ed) (1996) *Educating for Real*. Intermediate Technology Publications, London.

20   Quoted in James, R (2003) 'A legacy of swans left to science'. *The Observer*, 19 May.

21   For more discussion see *Crossroads* (1997–1998), the annual report of the Community Development Resource Association. Woodstock, South Africa.

22   Rist, G (1997) *The History of Development*. Zed Books, London, pp239–240.

23   Simmel, G (1971) *On Individuality and Social Forms*. The University of Chicago Press, Chicago IL, p155.

24   Goulet, D (1995) *Development Ethics*. ZED Books, London, p26.

25   Capra, F (2002) *The Hidden Connections, A Science For Sustainable Living*. Harper Collins, London, p124.

26   Edwards, M (2000) *NGO Rights and Responsibilities. A New Deal for Global Governance*. The Foreign Policy Centre in association with The National Council for Voluntary Organizations (NCVO), London, p29.

27   As reported by Lemann, N (2002) 'The next world order'. *New Yorker*, April 2002.

28   Memo from David Sanderson re: CARE Research Report on Urban Governance for Istanbul + 5, 6–8 June 2001.

29   As reported in *The Guardian*, 24 October 2003.

30   Rist, G (1997) *The History of Development*. Zed Books, London, p6.

PART 2: ENCOUNTERS IN PRACTICE

1   Nina's story on eviction and resettlement is based on interviews with residents in Bangkok, conducted in January 2002.

2   As reported in the newsletter of the Asian Coalition for Housing Rights, *Housing by People*, 12 (April 1999): 29. The eviction hotline was developed by the Thai Community Network to handle evictions nationwide.

3   Beall, J and Kanjil, N (1999) 'Households, livelihoods and urban poverty'. Theme paper (unpublished), commissioned by the Economic and Social research Unit of the Department for International Development (ESCOR) on urban development: Urban Governance, Partnerships and Poverty.

4   Patama's story is adapted from 'Santitham community: action planning design workshop in Chiangmai, Northern Thailand'. *OpenHouse International*, 24 (3) (1999): 40–47, and from interviews conducted in Thailand and Oxford.

5   Mela's story is based on that of Malani Jayalath, a community leader of Badowila, a settlement in Dehiwala Mt Livinia Municipality in Sri Lanka whom I interviewed in Sri Lanka in 2001.

6   Seva's involvement throughout is based on the work of the NGO Sevanatha. The composting bin was developed by Sevanatha as part of their Sustainable Colombo Core Area Project and was funded by NORAD. This story is based on interviews and on a report prepared for Sevanatha entitled *Composting Bins As An Alternative Solution*, by Prema Kumara (2000).

7   For a more detailed summary of both the Khonkaln Recycling Centre in Thailand and the Payatas Scavengers Association in The Philippines, see the newsletter of the Asian Coalition for Housing Rights, *Housing by People*, 12 (April 1999): 3–4.

8   Kaplan, A (1996) *The Development Practitioner's Handbook*. Pluto Press, London, p107.

9   Sustainable Urban Development (2001) *A Regional Perspective on Good Urban Governance*. UN Economic and Social Commission for Western Asia, New York, p11.

10 United Nations – Economic and Social Commission for Western Asia (ESCWA) (2001) *Sustainable Urban Development. A Regional Perspective on Good Urban Governance*, United Nations, New York, p15.

11 International Council on Human Rights (2003) *Enhancing Access to Human Rights*. Draft report for consultation, June 2003, Versoix, Switzerland, p40.

12 Sennett, R (2003) *Respect, The Formulation of Character in an Age of Inequality*. Allen Lane, The Penguin Press, London, p91.

13 Sennett (2003) ibid, p90.

14 Sennett (2003) ibid, pp89, 90.

15 Zohar, D (1997) *Rewiring The Corporate Brain*. Berrett-Koehler, San Francisco CA, p9.

16 Zohar, D (1997) *Rewiring The Corporate Brain*. Berrett-Koehler, San Francisco CA, p53.

17 Fishman, R (1972) *Urban Utopias in the Twentieth Century: Ebenezer Howard, Frank Lloyd Wright, Le Corbusier*. MIT Press, Cambridge MA, p254.

18 Harvey, D (1996) *Justice, Nature and the Geography of Difference*. Blackwell, London, quoted by Morgan, S in 'Work in progress' toward Master of Philosophy degree at the Architectural Association (February/March 1999) (unpublished).

19 For a full and detailed description and analysis of Community Action Planning see: Hamdi, N and Goethert, R (1997) *Action Planning for Cities. A Guide to Community Practice*. John Wiley & Sons, Chichester.

20 Baross, P (1991) *Action Planning*. Institute for Housing and Urban Development Studies, Rotterdam, Working Paper No. 2, p4.

21 Baross (1991) ibid, p15.

22 Baross (1991) ibid, p19.

23 Twigg, J (2002) 'The right to safety: an introduction'. Unpublished paper prepared for CARE International (UK)'s Mainstreaming Mitigation to Reduce Urban Risk Project, funded by DfID.

24 This process was developed for CARE International (UK)'s project 'Mainstreaming Mitigation to Reduce Urban Risk' and piloted in Jalashewar in Kathmandu, Mumbai and Ahmadabad in India. The examples used here to illustrate the process are based on the issues and needs in Jalashewar.

25 Harvey, D (1989) *The Condition of Post-modernity*. Basil Blackwell, Oxford, pp5, 66–67, quoting Raban, J (1974) *Soft City*. Hamish Hamilton, London.

26 Ghafur, S (2001) 'Beyond homemaking'. *Third World Planning Review*, 23 (2): 125.

27 Freeman, A, Pickup, F and Rashid, L (1997) 'Women's income – generating activities in the informal sector'. In Beall, J (ed) *A City for All*. Zed Books, London, p52.

28 Ghafur, S (2001) 'Beyond homemaking'. *Third World Planning Review*, 23 (2): 125.

29 Freeman, A, Pickup, F and Rashid, L (1997) 'Women's income – generating activities in the informal sector'. In Beall, J (ed) *A City for All*. Zed Books, London, p55.

30 Ghafur, S (2001) 'Beyond homemaking'. *Third World Planning Review*, 23 (2): 125.

31 Newsletter of the Asian Coalition for Housing Rights, *Housing by People*, 12 (April 1999): 28.

32 Sennet, R, quoted in Ward, C (1990) *Talking Houses*. Freedom Press, London, p85.

33 Capra, F (2002) *The Hidden Connections, A Science for Sustainable Living*. Harper Collins, London, p72.

34 Raban, J (1974) *Soft City*. Hamish Hamilton, London, p163.

35 Hillary, G A (1955) 'Definitions of community, areas of agreement', *Rural Sociology*, 20(2): 111–123.

36 Quoted in Anderson, N (1960) *The Urban Community*. Routledge and Kegan Paul, London, p25.

37 Anderson (1960) ibid, p26.

38 Capra, F (2002) *The Hidden Connections, A Science for Sustainable Living*. Harper Collins, London, p76.

39 Capra, F (2002) *The Hidden Connections, A Science for Sustainable Living*. Harper Collins, London, pp94, 95.

40 Morgan, S, 'Work in progress' toward Master of Philosophy degree at the Architectural Association (February/March 1999) (unpublished) and quoting Hooks, B, p28.

41 Thich, N H, quoted in Morgan (February/March 1999) ibid, p33.

42 Donnason, D (1993) 'Listen to the voice of the community'. Quoted in Sihlongonyane, M F (2001) 'The rhetoric of the community in project management: the case of Mohlakeng township'. *Development in Practice*, 11 (1) (February): 34.

43 Sihlongonyane, M (2001) ibid, quoting Guijt, I and Shah, M K (eds) (1993) *The Myth of Community*, IIED, London.

44 Beresford, J (1996) 'Now you see it, now you don't'. *Community Development Journal*, 31 (2): 137–142.

45 Bauer, R (2000) 'Building communities workshop Phnom Penh, Cambodia'. Reflective essay (unpublished).

46 Morgan, S, 'Work in progress' toward Master of Philosophy degree at the Architectural Association (February/March 1999) (unpublished) p10.

47 Johnson, S (2001) *Emergence: The Connected Lives of Ants, Brains, Cities and Software*. Allen Lane, The Penguin Press, London, p15.

48 Peattie, L P (1968) 'Reflections on advocacy planning'. *American Institute of Planners Journal*, 34 (2): 80–88.

49 See *One Day Bank Programme*. Annual Report 1996/1997, produced by Sevanatha.

50 For a more detailed description, see Wakeley, P et al (2001) *Implementing The Habitat Agenda. In Search of Urban Sustainability*. Development Planning Unit (DPU), London, pp44–45.

51 Adapted from the Participatory Hygiene and Sanitation Transformation (PHAST) undertaken in the Maili Saba settlement Kenya. Reported in *KIT* – the newsletter of the Intermediate Technology Development Group – Eastern Africa, September 2002.

52 Mayo, E and Moore, H (2001) *The Mutual State*. New Economics Foundation, London, p16.

53 'Empowering the community wealth for all'. *Botanic Gardens Conservation International* (December 1998).

PART 3: LEARNING PRACTICE

1 Dhu'l Nun in: Perry, W N (1971) *A Treasure of Traditional Wisdom*, George Allen and Unwin, London.

2 Kaplan, A (1996) *The Development Practitioners' Handbook*. Pluto Press, London, p74.

3 Illich, I (1973) *Tools for Conviviality*. Calder and Boyars, London, pxii.

4 Berger, P L and Neuhaus, R (1977) *To Empower People – The Role of Mediating Structures in Public Policy*. American Enterprise Institute for Public Policy Research, Washington DC, pp2, 3.

5 Schumacher, E F (1973) *Small is Beautiful: A Study of Economics as if People Mattered*. Abacus, London, pp53, 54.

6 Fishman, R (1982) *Urban Utopias in the Twentieth Century*. MIT Press, Cambridge, Mass.

7 Turner, J F C (1976) *Housing By People: Towards Autonomy in Building Environments*. Marion Boyers, New York.

8 Waldrop, M (1993) *Complexity: The Emerging Science at the Edge of Order and Chaos*. Touchstone Books, New York.

9 Capra, F (2002) *The Hidden Connections, A Science for Sustainable Living*. Harper Collins, London, p102.

10 Capra (2002) ibid, p105.

11 Hamdi, N (1995) *Housing Without Houses: Participation, Flexibility, Enablement*. Intermediate Technology Publications, London, p103.

12 Goulet, D (1995) *Development Ethics. A Guide to Theory and Practice*. Zed Books, London.

13   Yates, D (1980) *The Ungovernable City*. The MIT Press, Cambridge MA.

14   Turnbull, S (2002) *A New Way to Govern*. New Economics Foundation, London, p32.

15   Sennet, R, quoted in Ward, C (1990) *Talking Houses*. Freedom Press, London, p83.

16   Edwards, M (2001) 'The rise and rise of civil society'. *Developments*, 14: 7.

17   Mayo, E and Moore, H (2001) *The Mutual State*. New Economics Foundation, London, pp1, 6

18   Brinkerhoff, J M (2002) *Partnership for International Development*. Lynne Rienner, Boulder CO, p14.

19   Brinkerhoff (2002) ibid, p15.

20   Rakodi, C (1999) 'Tackling urban poverty: principles and practice in project and programme design'. Paper (unpublished) to the Seminar on From Welfare to Market Economy, Oxford Brookes University, 6 July 1999.

21   Capra, F (2002) *The Hidden Connections, A Science for Sustainable Living*. Harper Collins, London, p94.

22   Capra, F (2002) *The Hidden Connections, A Science for Sustainable Living*. Harper Collins, London, p14.

23   Khor, M (2001) *Rethinking Globalization*. Zed Books, London, p121.

24   Monbiot, G (2003) *The Age of Consent*. Flamingo, London.

25   Edwards, M (2000) *NGO Rights and Responsibilities*. The Foreign Policy Centre, London, p14.

26   Goulet, D (1995) *Development Ethics. A Guide to Theory and Practice*. Zed Books, London, p180.

27   Goulet, D (1995) *Development Ethics. A Guide to Theory and Practice*. Zed Books, London.

28   Edwards, M (1996) 'The getting of wisdom: educating the reflective practitioner'. In Hamdi, N (ed) *Educating for Real*. Intermediate Technology Publications, London, p21.

29   Goulet, D (1995) *Development Ethics. A Guide to Theory and Practice*. Zed Books, London.

30   *Chambers English Dictionary*.

31   Waldrop, M (1993) *Complexity: The Emerging Science at the Edge of Order and Chaos*. Touchstone Books, New York, p238.

32   Jacobs, J (1961) *The Death and Life of Great American Cities*, Random House, New York.

33   Hamdi, N (1996) 'A new orthodoxy in education', in Hamdi, N (ed) *Educating for Real*. Intermediate Technology Publications, London, p5.

34 Fuller, B R (1959) *No More Second Hand God*. Feffer & Simons, Inc, London, p52.

35 Raymond, M (2002) *Emergency Field Worker Skills*. Mann, p145.

36 Bauer, R (2000) 'Building communities workshop, Phnom Penh'. A reflective essay (unpublished).

37 Edwards, M (1996) 'The getting of wisdom: educating the reflective practitioner'. In Hamdi, N (ed) *Educating for Real*. Intermediate Technology Publications, London, p19.

38 Schon, D A (1984) *The Reflective Practitioner: How Professionals Think in Action*. Basic Books, New York, p50.

39 Zohar, D (1997) *Rewiring The Corporate Brain*. Berrett-Koehler, San Francisco CA, p35.

40 Schon, D A (1984) *The Reflective Practitioner: How Professionals Think in Action*. Basic Books, New York, pp296, 297.

41 Rahman, M A (1995) 'Participatory development: toward liberation or co-optation?'. In Craig, G and Mayo, M (eds) *Community Empowerment*. Zed Books, London, p25.

42 Simmel, G (1971) *On Individuality and Social Forms*. The University of Chicago Press, Chicago IL, p354.

43 Handy, C (1990) *The Age of Unreason*. Arrow Books, London, p199.

44 Handy (1990) ibid, p52.

45 Zohar, D (1997) *Rewiring The Corporate Brain*. Berrett-Koehler, San Francisco CA, p39.

46 Abt, C C (1970) *Serious Games*. The Viking Press, New York, p41.

47 Abt (1970) ibid, p5.

48 Abt (1970) ibid, pp11–13.

49 Kaplan, A (1996) *The Development Practitioners' Handbook*. Pluto Press, London, p74.

50 Handy, C (1990) *The Age of Unreason*. Arrow Books, London, p55.

51 Fox, J (2001) *Chomsky and Globalization*. Icon Books, Cambridge, p65.

52 Handy, C (1990) *The Age of Unreason*. Arrow Books, London, p55.

53 Richard Sennet, quoted in *The Guardian Review* 18 January 2003.

INDEX